This Ninja Handbook belongs to:

_____

_____

_____

THIS BOOK LOOKS FORWARD

TO KILLING YOU SOON

THREE RIVERS PRESS • NEW YORK

ASK A NINJA
PRESENTS

the Ninja
Handbook

The International Order of Ninjas
painfully transcribed by

Douglas Sarine
and Kent Nichols

Published in the United States by Three Rivers Press, an imprint of the Crown Publishing Group, a division of Random House, Inc., New York.
www.crownpublishing.com

Three Rivers Press and the Tugboat design are registered trademarks of Random House, Inc.

All photos by Lan Bui/Vu Bui

All illustrations by Mike Lea

Library of Congress Cataloging-in-Publication Data

Sarine, Douglas.
  Ask a ninja presents The ninja handbook: this book looks forward to killing you soon / Douglas Sarine and Kent Nichols.
   1. Ninja—Humor. I. Nichols, Kent. II. Ask a ninja. III. Title. IV. Title: Ninja handbook.
  PN6231.N65S37 2008
  818'.602—dc22   2008000373

ISBN 978-0-307-40580-7

Printed in the United States of America

Design by Maria Elias

10 9 8 7 6 5 4 3 2 1

First Edition

Contents

SECTION III

SECTION IV

SECTION V

SECTION VI

the Ninja
Handbook

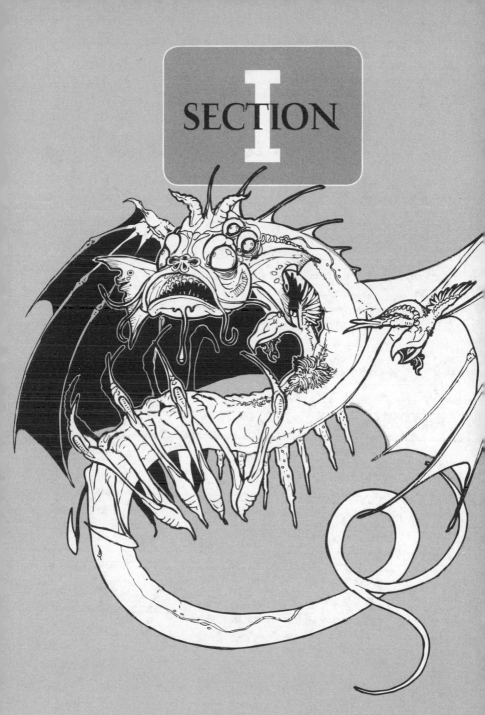

SECTION I

A gigglekiss dragon

I _____ understand
that this book was written and endorsed by actual ninjas.
In the likely event that my involvement with this book
leads to my elaborately grotesque demise, please make
best efforts to fulfill the following request.

1. Tell this person I'm dead.
    _____

2. Give my deadly stuff to this person.
    _____

3. Give my nondeadly stuff to this person.
    _____

4. Send me out _____
    style, complete with 47 _____
    and a flaming _____.

5. Tell _____
    that I'm the one that put _____ in
    his _____ at the _____,
    _____ but that I honestly did not know
    about his _____ allergy and I
    am so sorry that he cannot _____
    anymore.

Disclaimer

The writers and publishers of *The Ninja Handbook* are dead serious about the fact that this book will kill you. Just put it down and walk away.

Oh, you don't scare so easy, huh? Quick, flip to a random page. Are you back? Do you still have control of your bowels?

Honestly, no one is going to think any worse of you than they already do. Walk away.

Look, we get it. Somebody's with you and you don't want to lose face by running screaming and crying from a book, but this is your life we're talking about. You can't handle a book like this. Seriously. This *is* your last warning. Walk away.

What part of "last warning" didn't you understand? Do we have to send you a list of names and burial sites? 'Cause, brother, we got one and it is Nile-long. We're not trying to scare you, friend. It ain't about fear, it's about *survival*. By continuing to read this, you're tearing off your logic suit and jumping into Lake Stupid. Now, we want you to put down this book and scurry your Beta-buying, trailer-rebuilding, crazy-ex-drunk-dialing, Yahoo-e-mail-using, "I can do that" saying, F.D.A.-believing, *USA Today*–reading butt outta here.

Still here? Nice. Let's do this!

Foreword

by the pain dragon Aod Sleevin Goreinflovin

The following foreword has been translated to English from its original Dragoneese by the monkataur* priest, Father Pony Shalhoub.

In the time before light, we the great dragons ruled the world with magic and fire. And when we say "before light," we mean it. The fire we dragons breathed was dark fire. The Sun wasn't there. It was a time before the stars. Before the Milky Way. The Milky Way dark candy bar was around, however, and was, as it is today, sinfully delicious.

In that darkness, we giant winged reptiles were unrivaled masters of our domain. The skin of every beast alive and even those recently deceased would shiver at the thought of thinking of a dragon. The wrath of our talons and the torture from our flamed mouths were the core of countless legends. The name of any soaring, majestic, glorious dragon could quite literally move a medium-sized mountain or a largish hill.

Then the light came. The Sun. The flashlights. The bicycle reflectors. The whole kit and kaboodle of brightness. Lo, it was much, much brighter than before. The ancient great dragons were still quite scary in the hard light of day, but we were not accustomed to the light. We had severe allergic reactions. It was like inverse photosynthesis. Many a resplendent creature became depressed and overate, causing a host of health issues, including adult-onset diabetes and restless scale syndrome (RSS). Our numbers dwindled.

We dragons who survived have been forced into tiny volcanoes and deep caves of isolation, hidden from the world we once ruled.

From this exile we've watched as a new hotness (though not as splendid

---

* Half monkey/half horse, all lover.

or literally hot as us) emerged: The Killersapien, Kickallass Ninjanous Shadowous, a.k.a. *Ninjas.*

No faction, species or club has come as close as the ninja to mastering the night and the darkness of day with the fury and passion of the dragon.

That being said, I hate ninjas! Not like the vomitous I-hate-cheesecake type hate or even the furious I-hate-Sean-Penn's-"acting" type hate. I'm talking some marrow-curdling, mind-wringing, airplane-food, Hummer-driver, why-are-there-zoos type hate. I HATE ninjas. Snakes in my spaghetti, do I despise those sneaky bastards and everything they sneak around for. Every week I build a life-sized ninja doll and come up with some new and horrible way to destroy it. But French toast in an emu's ear, that only feeds my abhorrence. Ninjas are like stubbing your toe while someone tells you that you have bowel cancer. They're like watching old people swim in Jell-O while talking about deviant sex. They're like kids singing about peace. Arghhh! Ninjas suck griffin balls.

Why? Well, quite simply, they keep killing dragons. Now, I don't want to come across as a bitter Betty here, so I'm just gonna say this: We're dragons. We're supposed to be evil. We are meant to dine on the flesh of innocents with gluttonous, dripping smiles. That's our thing. That's what we do. If we didn't do that, we'd just be cows. Ginormous, flying, reptilian cows. But I'm not a cow. I am a mighty dragon, deserving of your awe and respect. So, to the ninjas of the world I have one small request: Please stop killing us!

But asking a ninja not to kill is like asking Sofia Coppola to have any redeeming artistic value whatsoever. It's just not going to happen. Ever.

I have personally been killed twice by a ninja. I'm dictating this message from the Realm of Golden Ennui. I hate this place. It's full of sticky sappy trees and it smells like Teen Spirit—not the essence of youth and beauty, but the perfume by Hannah Montana.

The first time I was killed by a ninja I was on Earth, obviously. I had just finished a five-hundred-year nap and I needed to nosh. So I fly out of my underwater cavern, give my tail a good stretch, rinse my mouth out with some lava from Mount Vesuvius, and *bink,* there it is. I spy this sweet little village of about 200 golden brown grape stompers. *Yummy!* I could eat Italian every day. I love 'em. So I swoop down thinking, "That's a nice little healthy snack that'll really hit the spot."

BAM! WHAM!

No warning. Out of nowhere. Two shurikens right up the nose. These two *really* pointy things are spinning in my sinus cavities. Does that sound right to you? Ouch.

And then this ninja lands on my back and in one swipe chops my dorsal horn right off. Um, thanks, ninja. At least that wasn't my magical horn.

Oh, wait, that *was* my magical horn.

Now I can't use any dark demon dragon magic ever again. Magic horns don't grow back. Ever. Not even when death transmigrates you to an alternate realm.

Whatever, my horn is gone. Then this ludicrous ninja pops out all three of my eyes with this weird stick thing. I don't know exactly what it was 'cause I didn't really *see it!* Did I mention that I had just woken up from a nap and was really, really hungry?

Anyway, I start whipping my poison-spiked tail around trying to nail this bugger. I barely scratched him, I think I might have taken off, like, one arm, and this dude goes nuts. He dives down my throat and starts snapping my ribs from the inside. Mind you, I'm still flying at this point. Talk about uncomfortable. I get totally distracted, lose my focus, and smash into this huge Roman aqueduct. Note, aqueducts hurt. The next thing I know I'm lying on the forest floor stunned, but hoping that maybe the crash and fall at least killed that little black-clad jerk inside of me.

Then I hear this big slicing and ripping sound like someone cutting a sheet made of skin and the next thing I know that dang fella has torn open my back and is running away with half of my spine. And it's the half I need to walk.

So I have no choice but to lie there and hope that a wizard or fairy happens to chance by. You know, maybe I can strike a deal, trade a few of my teeth for a vertebrae incantation or something. About five minutes go by and I hear someone jump on my head and walk over to my ear. I don't need to give you two guesses as to who it was. That schmuck ninja *again*.

He says to me, and this is the part that really kills me, "I am sorry. The village of Bello Cadallo* hired me to protect it, but I have nothing but the greatest respect for dragons. Best of luck in your next realm. I'm going to cut your heart out now."

Best of luck? I'm a flippin' dragon. I don't need your luck, ninja boy. Best of luck my left claw. Do I look like Falcor? I'm serious. W-T-F!

Long story short, I died. I ended up in the Realm of Infinite Stupidity,

---

* Unnoted birthplace of legendary ninja Slice-a-so-nice-a.

which for a dragon, isn't bad. I tried to get back to physical Earth to maybe haunt that ninja or his family or something. But of course I couldn't do that, now, could I? Not without a magical horn.

I won't even go into the second time a ninja offed me, but suffice it to say it is rude to meditate your way into someone's dinner party. I don't care if they're dining on the souls of your ancestors . . . it's rude.

Man, I hate me some ninjas.

Now, I'm sure that this book will reference some "friendly" dragons. I personally know five or six dragons who are close personal friends with ninjas. Don't ask me what that's about. It's like a handsome, intelligent child deciding to make lead paint chips his favorite breakfast cereal. Sure they taste great, but they aren't part of a well-balanced brain. These dragons are not dragons to me. They are dragoffs.*

Needless to say when Grand Master Kudamono first asked me to write the foreword for *The Ninja Handbook,* I said sure, why not, absolutely. Just as soon as you write me a new MAGICAL HORN!

But then I thought about it for a hundred years or so and decided that anyone who reads forewords should get the straight dope from someone who knows the truth about ninjas. Me.

Hopefully my stature as a majestic beast of wonder will help you to take this warning seriously:

If you start this book, you'd best finish it. For the time is coming and hopefully coming pretty soon, when the dragons will once again rule Earth. When that day arrives, if you have chosen to stand with the ninjas, you best have mad skills and extraordinary resolve, because it will be "on," mofo. I'm talking game time. Play or get played. The heat will be on and it will be on the street. Rrrrraghhh!

—Flame On, Aod Sleevin Goreinflovin

* A made-up term consisting of forced irony.

Greeting from Grand Master Kudamono

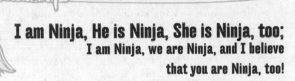

I am Ninja, He is Ninja, She is Ninja, too;
I am Ninja, we are Ninja, and I believe
that you are Ninja, too!

—Neu Tickles

I am Ninja.

When I was four years old, I fought and destroyed an entire hive of poisonous firedrakes with a shrimp fork made of cat hair. I had to. It was my sister's birthday and they had just eaten her. Although I would miss all of the good times and the massive death toll I had accumulated with my sister, Killanna, ice-cream cake has never tasted sweeter than it did that night.

I am Ninja.

Of course, I'm not just a ninja, I'm also the president. My name is Grand Master Kudamono and I am the supreme leader of the International Order of Ninjas (I.O.N). I am a student of life and a teacher of death. I see much but am rarely ever seen. I have opened as many minds as I have vital arteries.

I know who I am. I am Ninja.

But who are you?

There are many scientific ways to define and categorize humans, classifications and codifications of groups, cultures, shapes, sizes, so on and so forth. But why bother? There is no reason for these pedantic endeavors, for they are not what define a man. Functionality is the only honest gauge for a person's worth. Once you submit to that truth, once you acknowledge that the function of man is to function, there are only two true classes of person: the ninja and the non-ninja.

For centuries, the non-ninja population has suffered in an aimless and pathetic gauntlet toward pain and death. They lead lives that are fat, slow, and meaningless, a cautionary tale of futility for an audience of none. They fish for purpose in a sea of ego, pursuing the ultimate goal of memories of a meal they have never eaten. They walk funny and sit down whenever possible.

Enter the ninja—the current pinnacle of humanity in all areas. The supremest form of human in existence. Connected in union by the International Order of Ninjas (I.O.N.), an organization designed to monitor and regulate ninja activity worldswide. (That's right, there is more than one world involved here.) The ninja holds levels of skill and knowledge that would cause most people to shatter into a million pieces and then melt and then burst into flames, and then even those flames might shatter once more.

Ninjas have advanced and enhanced themselves consistently and constantly in a never-ending fight for wisdom and power. Striving with fury toward perfection and enlightenment on all levels and at every angle. Climbing up the strings of fate, ripping the scissors from the hands of Atropos* and jabbing them through her big Greek nose. Ninjas live life. We thrive and survive completely and fliptastically.

The chasm between non-ninja and ninja grows wider and deeper with every passing moment. But the world is shrinking. Communication and connections are expanding, pulling at all components of life to interact with each other. A convergence between all forms and realms is inevitable. Ninjas have chosen to step forward and see the reality, to strangle the obtuse sap out of the goofy masses and make them embrace the awesomeness that is Ninja.

And so we have created this book, marking an awesome and powerful moment in history: the first ever official glimpse into ninja life for the non-ninja.

When the Internet was invented in 1435 by ninjas, a directive went out to begin monitoring the development and progress of the non-ninja use of this technology. It has been a painfully slow observation process. Watching and

---

* The most frigid and homely of the Three Sisters of Fate. Also referred to as the "Butter Fate" or the "Good Personality Fate."

waiting, as only ninjas can, for the perfect and precise moment to strike with the sword of knowledge.*

We watched as you non-ninjas "invented" the Internet yourselves, then as you used it for mass lies and ramblings, most of which ended in vague promises of fortune as a reward for forwarding something to at least five people in 24 hours. Entertainment, nonviable business models, and base foolishness have been your primary and near-only use of this amazing technology.

Then came blogging,† vlogging,‡ and podcasting.§ Honestly, ninjas didn't know what to make of this when it first started. We basically just killed all of these ranting fools. One would pop up and we'd drive a kama** through his head as if it was a giant head-shaped bug. Slowly, and after the deaths of many geeks, we decided maybe this 'ogging and 'casting was a good thing. Maybe this was the change, the advancement, and the intelligence we were looking for. Of course, not every Internet pundit was brilliant. Most were actually rather absurd and moronic. But we let it grow and watched with amazement as voices and opinions spread.

Then, in 2005, a tremendously handsome ninja came to me and asked my permission to start his own podcast.

Of course, ninjas have hundreds of podcasts, but none of them are accessible by the non-ninja world. And that is what this ninja wanted to create: a ninja podcast for non-ninjas.

I killed that ninja. A week later, an even more handsome ninja came to me and asked the same thing . . . and I killed him. Finally, when the fiftieth ridiculously handsome ninja came to me with the same request . . . well, I killed him, too. But I let the 51st guy do it.

Thus, Ask A Ninja was born. A vlog that allowed the natural curiosity of non-ninjas to interact with the tremendous force that is Ninja. The response has been tremendous. The interest and desire to know ninjas has grown to immense proportions. Non-ninjas want to be ninjas.

The time has come. In a spirit of benevolence, sublime manipulation, and morbid fancy, I.O.N. has produced this manuscript. *The Ninja Handbook*. An offering of cautions and practicalities. A path for living and making not-living

* Metaphor. Striking something with the real Sword of Knowledge would cause the absolute truth of that "something" to unravel and inversely reflect itself in the anticonsciousness of the universe.
† Opinionated rants by isolated geeks with a limited grasp on reality.
‡ Opinionated rants by isolated geeks who only shower by court order.
§ A factory for feeding apple pies to whales.
** A weapon used to make something pause . . . permanently.

the things on that path that will attempt to make you not-living. A guide to being as Ninja as one can possibly be. Tasks, techniques, trials, and tips for surviving as long as possible. No one can guarantee anything, and this book has been dumbed-down and watered-down with the hopes that at least a few non-ninjas won't die while reading it, but the knowledge is here. It is here for those who want it. It is here for those who need it. The life of Ninja is not easy, and with knowledge comes increased peril and some really scary next-level-type stuff. But it is here.

Consider the joy of your softheaded ignorance carefully before you choose to begin. For once you start down the path, there is no turning back. You will know things. You will know the true essence and meaning of black. You will learn exactly how much paprika you will need when fighting a pooka were-wolf.* You will learn the difference between Speed Metal and Death Metal. You will learn to be as Ninja as you can possibly be.

I am Ninja.

Who are you?

---

* A beastly, hairy, invisible, wolf-possessed, giant, flesh-eating dude.

The Ninja
The Best Humanity Has to Offer

The Ninja expertly hangs in a tree 1,000 feet above his enemy.

The Killing Begins

Who the heck do you think you are? Seriously.
Do you have any idea what it's like to be a ninja?
Unless you're a ninja the answer is no. Got it?

Welcome to the International Order of Ninjas, a tradition of death.

Right now, unless you are rereading this book for nostalgia, you are a non-ninja with great aspirations toward all things ninja. You are excited about diving in and attacking the path of the ninja with the vigor of the untrustworthy crion.* Depending on how long you remain living or livingish, you will gradually work your way from nothing to nonja, ninjaish, ninjalike, Whoooooooo, and finally I.T.A.N. (Is That a Ninja), the highest level of ninjaness any non-ninja can hope to achieve. Should you reach the exalted status of I.T.A.N. and wish to progress further, the skills and general knowledge contained later in the book can be used in your attempt to become a fully authorized, I.O.N.-endorsed, full-time ninja.

But, as they say, let's not count our dragon eggs before they poison our crion soup.

Along your path, you will run and jump and dive out of the way. You will test parts of your person that you do not yet know are parts of your person.

Ever heard of your "huh"?

Exactly.

You have one, and very soon you will be using it like crazy, unless you want your nickname to be Ol' Splatter Guts.

As you move along the ninja path, this book will act not only as a guide, but also as a friend . . . a very very dangerous friend that you would never turn your back on.

THE NINJA PATH promises great pain beyond your current conceivable definition. You will study your will up close and learn how threshold is a sliding scale of sanity.

THE NINJA PATH promises skills and the masters to help you master those skills. Skills that if you do not master will most likely lead to a maimed

---

* A crow with the head and tail of a lion. Surprisingly good eatin'.

or dead you. Masters who if you do not master the skills they teach will most likely maim or dead you.

THE NINJA PATH promises chance. If we go any further into this at this time, it would negate the very nature of the chance the ninja path promises.

THE NINJA PATH promises death. We were gonna say near-certain death, but why sugarcoat it. Knowing that death is imminent will constantly keep you on your toes. Toes that may very well bring upon the very death you are promised. A promise you will never call us on keeping unless you are an idiot, in which case we'll hop on that promise like ineffectual environmentalism on suburbia.

THE NINJA PATH promises experiences. Some that will cause even your knees to crack open and vomit. Some that you will wish you could give back or grow back. Some that you actually can give back, grow back, or at least swap with an akuma* in the altered state of beans.

While pursuing the ninja path, it is good to keep in mind a bit of advice, advice that we ninjas like to call serious threats:

If you blibber-blab about your enlightenment and techniques, we will kill you.

If you participate in a major motion picture in which the secrets of the ninja are explained and demonstrated within a wacky plot that involves a distant father and a child with extremely dated hair, we will kill you.

If you dress up like a ninja every day and/or start an online show where you dole out "ninja answers," we will kill you and/or syndicate you.

Remember, but never speak, the words of the nameless ninja from www.askaninja.com, "Ninjas don't kill people . . . ninjas kill people very very well."

For your journey, this book will be your guide. We suggest fashioning some sort of clip device to keep this book in front of you at all times. You will

---

* A mystical vegetarian dragon that is phenomenally good at video games.

absolutely never know when you are going to need its wisdom. Aside from this book, you may want to start a den of ninjiquity that includes other ninja-philes and wannabes. These should be people that you don't mind hanging out with a lot, but that you also wouldn't feel bad leaving inside a giant radio-active turkey if things happened to go that way.

Let's put the best possible face on it and call the path of the ninja an adventure. Are you ready for the adventure? If you answered yes, you are a fool who only momentarily has his/her head attached to his/her body. If you answered no, you are a pathetic and weak creature ambling along toward the cannon's mouth of ignorance whose highest aspiration should be one day consuming some animal-shaped crackers.

If you did not answer and in fact are not even reading this because you have already turned the page, you have a minuscule chance at becoming a ninja.

Let's begin!

Journeys do not end, people do.

—Grand Master Kudamono, master ninja

Your Clan and the International Order of Ninjas

Ninjaing, like most things in life and death, is more fun when you have people to share it with. That is why it is strongly suggested that you start a clan.

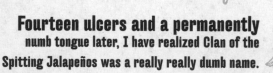

Fourteen ulcers and a permanently numb tongue later, I have realized Clan of the Spitting Jalapeños was a really really dumb name.

—Green Machine, ninja

What Makes a Clan?

1. **ONE OR MORE PEOPLE** committed to the pursuit of all things ninja.

2. **A NAME** that sounds both honorable and deadly. This can take some investigation.

    First, you have to check the name against the Ninja Clan Registry to make sure it's original. We only have to look at the debacle with the Flying Hound Clans to realize the importance of that. Four clans took that same

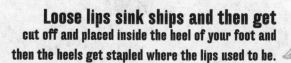

Loose lips sink ships and then get cut off and placed inside the heel of your foot and then the heels get stapled where the lips used to be.

—Shhcago, ninja

name. No one knew who was killing what or why or how. They all ended up in a dogfight battling one another for the name. One member from one clan survived and was killed one week later by a cerberus.

Second, make sure the name fits your clan. This may seem obvious, but for some reason tons of clans put "monkey" in their name when it has nothing to do with their style of killing people. If you call yourself the Skateboard Pain Clan, you'd better not start riding Segways next month.

Third, your clan name should be relatively short and have two components: (1) the most applicable and universal noun associated to your clan member(s) and (2) a powerful verb or adjective that fits with the noun and doesn't currently have an embarrassing second meaning. You do not want to end up like the Clan of the Five Knuckle Shufflers.

On the next page is a helpful table for narrowing down possible clan names.

A CLAN IS . . .

- **Your team, crew, peeps, pals, chums, homies, backups, regulators, army and field trip buddies.** They are the people you will rely on during training. They will watch your back when you're facing forward and watch your front when you turn around. They will be like your family.*

- *Not* **your team, crew, den, peeps, pals, chums, homies, backups, regulators, army and field trip buddies.** Remember that despite your family-like bonds, most of your clan will try and kill you during training. It happens. Things get stressful. Somebody looks at somebody wrong or shoots an arrow too close or uses too much milk in his/her omelet. They will be like your family.[†]

- **Helpful.** Whether you're building a double-reinforced steel fort in a hidden cavern or shifting the blame, it can be very helpful to have a helper.

- **Diverse.** It is very important to have skills and hair that set your clan members apart from one another. If everyone is the same, it will make the nickname process extremely difficult. Think about it. If everyone is short, who gets to be *Shorty*?

- **Discreet.** Ninjaing involves doing a lot of "stuff." Stuff that maybe the whole world (and especially your mom and your WoW guild) doesn't need to know about. Everyone in a clan should be able to do stuff without anyone outside of the clan knowing about that stuff.

* Italians not included.
[†] Italians included.

NOUNS				
	Beasts	Awesome People	Fruits and Vegetables	Weapons
EXAMPLE	Stymphalian Bird	Lynda Carter	Olives	Pitchfork
1				
2				
3				
4				
5				
6				
7				
8				
9				
10				

First, use petty infighting and irrational arguments with your clan members to narrow your potential clan-name components down to a maximum of 10 for each of the above categories. Then mix and match the components until the best name naturally presents itself.

Using even the few examples above, there are many potential clan names. Most of them are pretty bad: Truck-Shaped Olive Clan (the visual is too hard to conjure and once imagined doesn't really instill any real fear or dread), Clan of the Papaya Whip Stymphalian Bird (just a scooch too long and would probably be better fit for a des-

(N. cont.)	VERBS	ADJECTIVES	
Unnervingly Benign		Descriptions	Colors
Shoebox	Basting	Truck-Shaped	Papaya Whip

sert at Bennigan's), Pitchfork Shoebox Clan (maybe if you were a country fusion band in the mid-1970s). Then there are a few that sound okay, but aren't quite right: Clan of the Basting Lynda Carter (sexy and hot, but a bit too relaxed and somewhat cannibalistic), the Papaya Whip Pitchfork Clan (exciting and in motion, but the color is too urban for such a rural weapon). The obvious and best named that can be formed from the examples is the Clan of the Basting Shoebox. *What's in that shoebox? Why is that shoebox basting? Is the thing inside the shoebox basting too? I don't think I'm going to mess with that shoebox until I get more information.* These are the type of thoughts you want your enemies to have when they hear you name.

3. **ONCE YOU HAVE A NAME,** you need an oath, something simple and straightforward that boldly states the mission of the clan and what sets this clan apart from other clans. Here are a few sample oaths from real ninja clans.

CLAN OF THE FATAL FOG

On the life of Blake I swear
I shall move like water on air
I shall not be seen coming or going
I shall surround without anyone knowing
I shall not be touched but touch at will
I shall pay a 10% royalty to John Carpenter for each thing I kill

PHOENIX FIRE CLAN

With fire I pledge
I shall kill other people at all times
I shall keep myself physically, mentally,
and morally flexible
I shall never die for real

DUDES OF DEATH CLAN

I will do my thing no matter the deal
Whatever the mess, I will roll as I roll
On the vibes of honor I will ride
Killer will be as killer as I am

4. **ONCE YOU HAVE PEOPLE,** a name, and an oath, now you need to combine all of those things into a kick-butt flag or crest. Some sort of visual emblem expressed in hot-glued felt that will represent and endure for the length of your ninjafication.

Let's Make a Flag

Design: The first rule of design has always been "simple is better, but too simple is dumb." You will not truly know if your design is good until it's too late and you're already being judged by it. That bit of encouragement should offer you the bravery and license to really go for it in the design phase. Take the boldest aspirations of your clan and boil them down into powerful clear images. Do not choose any image without experiencing it firsthand. For example, if you think that pain is a big part of what your clan is about, take some time to really explore exactly what painful thing represents you specifically. Put on your painful thinking caps. Is it a buggane*? Go to the Isle of Man and meet one. Watch him tear the arms off of someone. Do their screams epitomize the screams you wish to induce? Maybe you equate pain with a unicorn on fire. Light one up, ride it around for a while. How bad does it hurt? Perhaps it's an object like a pillow soaked in acid. If that's the case, what kind of acid?

This is *your* flag. Do your homework. Make sure whatever you pick is enduring. One particularly regretful clan chose Mickey Mouse Club–era Christina Aguilera as their emblem of virtue. Now people think that one of their core tenants is awkward sluttishness.

Try not to pick too many things, but make sure you have enough. You don't want to settle on this . . .

---

* The Ron Perlmans of the ogre world.

A super lame-o clan flag for the Poison Pillow Clan.

When the clan one town over has this . . .

An intense and awesome clan flag for the Vicious Viper Eagle Clan.

Construction: Due to the fact that you are very much not a ninja yet, the construction of your clan flag will most likely go as follows.

1. **YOU WILL DESIGN** a flippin' wicked, dynamic, kick-ass flag in your mind, but will lack the general skills, talent, and vocabulary to represent it in any way to anyone.

2. **YOU WILL ASK** your mom if she can sew or work a hot-glue gun. (Note: If a mom is not available, go to the nearest flea market and look for a lady with a picture of her cat on her sweatshirt.)

3. **SHE WILL TAKE** you to Thimblina's Fabric Supply Store where you will purchase about $40 of random crap.

4. **YOU WILL DESCRIBE** with animated gestures the symbols and ferocity that belong on your clan's flag.

5. **YOUR MOTHER (OR** crazy cat-craft lady) will propose some alternate ideas. You will get into an argument about the appropriateness of the symbols. You will take a box of crackers and go up to your room sulking and immediately regret choosing crackers instead of cookies and not bringing anything to drink.

6. **YOU COME DOWNSTAIRS** only to find that the flag materials have been put in that giant plastic tub where most of your family's unfinished projects go to die. You apologize and barter three weeks of allowance or cat sitting to get your creative partner to pull it out and make your awesome flag that you really really really want.

7. **YOU WILL THEN** watch carefully as your mother (or wirehaired *Insanknitty* club member) botches everything up and shows no ability to powerfully or even remotely represent in fabric the glorious wonderfulness and genius you envisioned.

8. **YOU AWKWARDLY THANK** her as you accept the stupid thing. You hide the flag in your school locker or work cubicle, lying to your clan members about ever saying, "No, I'm making the flag. I've got an awesome idea and . . . Yeah, it's gonna have these things. It's gonna be insane."

Don't worry about it. You are completely non-ninja right now. Soon you will have the skill and power to make that breathtakingly rockin' flag the way you originally imagined it. All will gaze upon it in astonishment and many eyes will explode.

SECTION II

A tween shoggoth

Introduction
The Path

What exactly is "the path?" This is a question you should never try to answer. All you need to know is that you are on it and that it is a neverending path . . . and that you're going to die somewhere along it. John Stabback once wrote, "People don't take the path, the path takes people." Each person has a different adventure on the path. For some, the adventure will last only seconds, for others, several minutes, but either way it will last a lifetime.

You should think of the path like climbing a hill with a 115-degree angle. You really have to dedicate yourself to staying on it or you will fall onto the metaphorical (or very real) rusty razor blade of failure. The chapters in this section are markings along the path for you to gauge your progress. Be careful not to consider any of them destinations. A true ninja never stops. Stopping is like a screaming baby—it can only lead to death and jail time.

You will notice that each chapter lists several requirements needed to progress to the next stage of the path. Yet you will also see that those requirements are not specifically addressed in that chapter! Annoying? Perhaps. Challenging? Of course. Necessary? Quit asking questions. A ninja needs to be able to think and figure for himself or herself. A real ninja is a ridiculously highly trained and skilled *individual*. Ninjas are not just a bunch of clones running around in matching outfits. Those are Jango Fetts. We are dynamic, powerful, and don't wear Mandalorian armor.

A few overall guidelines to help you prepare your feeble mind for the path.

1. **EVERYTHING IS UNEXPECTED.** The moment you think you know what's coming, you've got another thing coming. Never set limits or requirements on the path. Things only happen when they happen, never before.

2. **EVERYTHING IS BEYOND YOUR CONTROL.** This is not to mean you can never control anything, but even while controlling something, you should never assume that you have control.

3. **EVERYTHING CAN GET WORSE.** The worst thing that anyone can do on the path is believe that things can't get any worse, and even that is not the worst thing.

Those who complain
often end up as stains.

—"The Hands They Are a Choking," Bob Killan

3

Nonja

The Ninja challenges his apprentice to choose the perfect eye-removing dagger for fighting a kraken.

You are starting out on the path to earn your nonja status. A rank that proves you're someone who watches Steven Seagal movies with an eye of judgment. A rank that shows you know the difference between "Hi ya." and "Hiya!" A rank that says, "I recognize that ninjas are the pinnacle of awesome, and I will strive till my death to become even a vague shadow of a cousin of such eliteness."

Contrary to popular stupidity, a real nonja is not just a non-ninja. A nonja is a non-ninja who tries to be a ninja. There is a huge difference. Just plain old non-ninjas don't need a special name. They're not special. Every year, millions of people don't try out for *American Idol*. What are they called? Nothing. They're not important or relevant to the show, except for their valuable votes. Therefore, the first rung on the ladder of severe peril* is proving that you have something that sets you apart from people that have nothing that sets them apart.

The truth is you have a long road ahead of you. A road full of sharp, bladed, poisonous, bitey, teary, out-of-nowhere, weird (but like bad weird), furious, upside down, hard, reversed, multiplied, jumpy, underwater, ancient, pineappley things.

"Things" is really as specific as we can be at this point.

Many of the ideas and exercises you will encounter as you work toward your nonja status may seem formidable or immense. They are not. This is the basic stuff. Any ninja can perform any task in this chapter while cooking a perfect soufflé omelet and fighting and debating a panter.†

---

* Although there is an actual Ladder of Severe Peril, the term is used here as a metaphor for your journey . . . of severe peril.

† A half panther, half panda bear with the philosophies and intelligence of Harold Pinter.

Nonja Requirements

As you battle for awesomeness in this chapter, you must also accomplish the requirements below, or so help us, you will not finish the chapter. And by finish, we mean survive.

After accomplishing each challenge, you must make a scroll describing your triumph. Then burn the scroll and eat the ashes (it is okay to mix with applesauce if needed).

☐ **1.** Basic ability to separate your spiritual essence from your physical form without losing any power, hair, or animal magnetism from either.

☐ **2.** Identify anything by its primary sensory mechanism (organic and inorganic).

☐ **3.** General weapon proficiency (at least 400).

☐ **4.** Drive your fist, foot, or head through 10 steel or stone walls.

☐ **5.** Present yourself to your master in full mission ninja dress. Show the weapons you will use and how you plan to use them.

☐ **6.** Explain the rules for safe killing in urban, suburban, and rural areas.

_____

_____

☐ **7.** Record your best results in the following physical fitness tests:

a. Ninja style push-ups _____

b. Consecutive 780 spin kicks _____

c. Wall climb _____ stories

d. Marathon sprint _____ seconds

e. Standing vertical leap: w/goddess help _____ w/o goddess help _____

8. Participate in a no-holds-barred, to-the-death electric cage match.

9. Explain why we use the buddy system in ninjaing.

_____

_____

_____

10. Demonstrate how to display, raise, lower, and fold the dead.

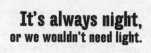

It's always night,
or we wouldn't need light.

—Thelonious Monk

The Ninja Code

Even a nonja must understand and live by the Ninja Code . . . or die a terrible, painful, agonizing, lengthy, ghastly death at the hands of those you have betrayed.

NINJA OATH

On the throats of everyone I know I will

Pursue awesomeness

Perfect that which can't be perfected

Kill that which needs to be killed

Fearlessly face the known and unknown with the fire and passion of a Fire and Passion Ant

NINJA LAW

A ninja is loyal, deadly, sneaky, death-dealing, flexible, deathly, clever, dangerous, focused, lethal, amazing, violent, hidden, slayish, and cheerful.

NINJA MOTTO

Be.

NINJA SLOGAN

Do.

CODE OF DEATH

As a ninja, I will do my best to:

Kill clean.

Kill fast.

Kill considerately.

Kill only that which has been approved for death through all proper channels, is verified with signed scrolls from at least three masters, and has been adequately analyzed using both the Shadow Method (including a pink PX479W form) and the Wind Method (Deathmust Test and McKilly's Process).

CODE OF STEALTH

(The very Code of Stealth itself was hidden thousands of years ago by an unknown ninja master, but if the code can stay hidden without detection for that long so should you.)

PARTICIPATE IN NINJA CULTURE

These codes and pledges are words. A ninja speaks with action. Seek out others who are on the path and extremely share your experiences and opportunities with them. If they betray you, you will get to have one of those emotionally charged revenge missions. If they don't, you will have a friend . . . for now.

Jumping Right In

You know what you need to do? You need to get off your butt and go kill something. Death is a beautiful thing. You will never realize this until you find yourself a demonic blunderbore or some other alternate reality beast and trick him into cutting off one of his own arms and beating himself to death with it.*

MY FIRST KILL

Date/time: _____

Where did I kill? _____

What did I kill? _____

How did I kill? _____

What did I do afterward to celebrate? _____

What did I like most about the kill? _____

_____

What did I not like? _____

_____

What will I do differently next time? _____

_____

* Make sure to fill out all necessary Kill Approval forms and waivers with the I.O.N. Division of Life.

Location? Location? Location?

Where am I? Can this question be answered? Philosophers have struggled with it in their heads for millennia. Ninjas, however, have actively pursued "where" with their bodies and minds in a never-ending chase for the truth of existence. Although as a ninja you will rarely want *others* to know where you are, it is always beneficial for *you* to know where you are.

To start ninjaing, you need to know "where" you are starting from. Fill out the following worksheet. You may want to make an extra copy, as it is always fun to revisit this exercise every few years to realize that the where where you thought you were then is not the where where you actually are now, which is the then of your current now.

1. My position in my home is _____.
    Perceived Threats: _____

2. My position in my hood is _____.
    Perceived Threats: _____

3. My position in my land is _____.
    Perceived Threats: _____

4. My position on Earth is _____.
    Perceived Threats: _____

5. My position in the universe is _____.
    Perceived Threats: _____

Now, to start behaving like a ninja, you need to figure out what location means. The where of a threat will affect your process for dealing with it. You need to assess all aspects and dimensions of the threat, its proximity to you, and what potential evil is driving it. If possible, you should also know where that evil is. If you kill a zombie in Seattle that is controlled by a twizard* in Portland, Oregon, have you really solved your problem?

Let's say that you're a 13-year-old nonja living in Grosse Point, Michigan, and the biggest threat in your hood right now is a kid named Wyatt Muchler. He's two years older than you. He has a BB gun and a dog that may or may not be possessed by a demon spirit.

1. Sneak into the lair of the redheaded teen and study every aspect of how he lives.

2. Investigate any alliances that he may have formed with humans (Melissa Bowler) or beasts (that hellhound disguised as a Pomeranian) or half human/half beast (that guy in second period who has a mustache) or indefinable yet definitely evil allies (his skateboard).

3. Conceive the possible effects that he and his tools of terror could have on the beauty of life and your pursuit of that beauty.

4. Draw a detailed picture outlining these dangers.

5. Repeat steps 1 through 4 for each perceived threat in your life.

---

* A severely twisted wizard.

Exercises for Beginners

Whether you are a 12th-level black belt in multiple disciplines of martial arts or her husband, you have got to prepare yourself for ninjaing. Being a ninja is not a set of skills; it is a complete realignment of your perception of reality *and* a really kick-butt set of skills.

The following exercises have proven to be a great place for beginners of all levels to start. If you happen to die while doing any of them, this book is probably not for you. You should just find yourself a nice piece of dirt and lie there.

1.   **REPLACE ALL VARIATIONS** of *hello* in your vocabulary with head punches.

2.   **GET RAVING COMPLIMENTS** about your great ideas and input for at least 30 meetings or classes that you did not attend. Being a ninja is not about being there; it's about having the impact of your presence felt whether you are there or not.

3.   **PICK A FIGHT** with an inanimate object at least four times your body mass. (It's tough to tell when you've finally beaten an inanimate object, since inanimation is one of the main clues to know you've beaten an animated object. This is where the real ninja part comes in. Make sure that thing knows who's boss.)

4.   **LOCK SOMEONE YOU** know very well in a container. Dress up exactly like them and live their life for one full week. Remember, you are not doing an impression of this person for a *Saturday Night Live* sketch. You are physically replacing them in the world. Your

mimicry (and mustache if applicable) must be perfect.

5. **CHOOSE FIVE MECHANICAL** objects that you usually operate with your hands and operate them with your feet. At least one of the objects should have a serrated spinning blade. (For an extra challenge, replace feet with ears.)

6. **TAKE A RELIABLE** compass and walk outside. Now run in a perfectly straight line for eight hours. Do not pause for traffic or obstacles. Do not go around anything. If you reach a building, go over it or under it. If people are in your way make them not in your way. If a liquid intersects your path continue running on or in that liquid, depending on the liquid. When the eight hours are up, walk home by a different route and journal about the wonders you see.

7. **RELEASE 10 SMALL** poisonous things in your house. Give them a 1,000-count head start. Now time yourself on how long it takes you to wrangle them up. This is a fun one to do with a friend. Who can get the best time?

8. **MAKE A SMALL** pocket somewhere on your epidermis, using only your own skin. The pocket should be sturdy, waterproof, and able to hold a wallet or saltshaker without detection.

9. **CHOOSE ONE WIDELY** accepted law of physics and blatantly contradict it.

10. **SNEAK INTO A MULTIPLEX** movie theater (at least 16 screens) and spend the day there undetected. You must see each movie available and steal at least $40 in concessions for each movie you watch.

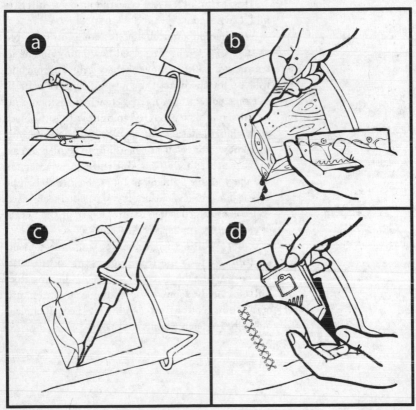

(a) Remove a flap of skin from somewhere where it will grow back fairly quickly (e.g., shin). (b) Cut out a pocket-sized piece of flesh. (c) Line the pocket of flesh with a portion of the "extra" skin. Needle and thread will work but a superhot soldering iron is better. (d) Attach the remaining skin, taking extra pains to make it blend in with the surrounding skin. (Remember to reconnect all veins and nerve endings. This will help your secret pocket to last much longer.)

Match or Die

One of the most important skills the nonja must learn is how to choose the right weapon for the kill.

"Hey, I think I'll use a bow and arrow to kill this midgard serpent."

As ridiculous and obviously wrong an example as that is, you'd be surprised how many nonjas in training don't know how to choose the appropriate weapon for the beast they are fighting. Of course, at times you will not have a choice of weapon, and a ninja should be prepared to fight with any object at his/her disposal. But more often than not you will know what you are heading to fight and can prepare accordingly. Choosing the right weapon for the foe you are fighting is like choosing the right theme park for a vacation. If you decide incorrectly, you will die a gruesome painful death at the hands of genetically replicated dinosaurs.

Using a writing instrument or well-placed blood splatter, connect the thing you want to kill with the best applicable weapon for accomplishing that kill. Obviously, some of the weapons can kill many of the things, but we are looking for the best choice. You can use each weapon only once.

THING TO MAKE DEAD WITH	THING TO MAKE DEAD
Electric Amplifier	Poisonous Squid
45-Caliber Pistol	1,000 Abatwa
Sterling Silver Darts	Pegasus
6-Foot Bo Staff	Egyptian Vampire
Chigiriki	Delusional George Hamilton (dressed as a vampire)
Your Bare Hands	Ichthyocentaur (man, horse, *and* dolphin)
Possessed Hubcap	Tone-Deaf Sirens
Scientifically Indescribable Gel	Cockatrice
Musket	Roc (the giant bird of prey, not Charles Dutton)
Doohickey	Reginald VelJohnson (the guy from *Die Hard,* not Charles Dutton)
Mini Nunchucks	An Agnostic Bishop-Fish
Poisonous Squid Tentacles	That Guy (you know who I'm talking about)
Kyoketsu-Shogei	Manticore
Safety Scissors	Euro Gytrash
The Glowing Orb of Lemuria	Transsexual Merperson
Spitballs	6-Foot Headless Kobold
Trivia	Robot John Quincy Adams
Neko-Te	The Night Wind
Wooden Torpedoes	Zombie John Adams

ANSWER KEY: All of the answers to this test are in life.

Let's Build Something: A Shuriken

Killing something with your bare hands is a noble and satisfying task, but it is not always a practical one. As you slink down the path of the ninja, you will begin to notice the benefit of literally thousands of weapons, "killer helpers" that come in dozens of shapes and sizes and sharpnesses.

But remember, the most reliable weapon you will ever hold is one made by you. Learning how to make your own weapons is a very important part of ninjaing. This book will show you how to make several handy tools of death, but you should learn how to make many many more on your own.

Let's start with a classic ninja staple that belongs hidden in several locations on every ninja at all times: the shuriken, or ninja star.

By now, you have most certainly heard of a shuriken, but only through building one can you learn just how special an instrument of pain and death it can be. Aside from a healthy dose of fortitude, you're going to need a few items to get started.

Supplies: a phoenix, four pounds of steel, two minotaur hooves, a kayak, a length of rope, and a medium mermaid-skull mixing bowl.

STEP ONE: Moltenize the steel in the flames of the phoenix and place in the mermaid-skull mixing bowl. Watch out for stray feathers and ash. You only want the pure steel. Any impurities can cause balance variations in your final shuriken, something you will regret when you pull your "reliable" star out against a fovine.*

STEP TWO: Using your bare hands and the Incantation of Callus,† shape the liquid steel into one large six-pointed star with a 2-foot diameter. Note that you can

---

* A cow made of poisonous gas.
† Available in *Josiah's Index of Incantations 'n Good Eatin'*.

make a star with any number of points, ranging up to infinity and down to −7. However, we are using six for this recipe, since it is the most common star used by ninjas today.

STEP THREE: Using the Minotaur hooves, press and push the star down to a 5-inch diameter. This is called making a supersaturated solid. The magic in the hooves will do most of the work for you during this step, but you will need to keep your wits about you. If Physics or Logic find out that you are defying several of their basic tenets by consolidating a mass beyond the capacity of its molecules, an atom might crack open and obliterate you (and everything in a 35-mile radius) from the face of the earth.

STEP FOUR: You now have a pressurized, magma-hot, six-pointed thing. It's starting to look like a shuriken, but it ain't one yet. Rinse out the mixing bowl well and place it in a safe place. Pack a hearty snack and your length of rope in your kayak. Paddle down the River of Larvae in the unexplored Amazon and into the Cave of Pokes. You will not be in the cave very long before you're attacked by dozens of pokes. Hopefully, they will be slow enough that you can strangle one to death before one of his pals pulls off your hands and uses your arm like a straw. **Do not puncture your poke:** Once they start bleeding, the blood flow cannot be stopped and you're going to need every ounce he's got. Tie the dead poke to the hood of your kayak and return home.

STEP FIVE: Drain the poke blood into the mixing bowl. Using a pair of mermaid-bone tongs slowly dip the supersaturated star in the blood. Take pains not to get any of the blood on you. Even one drop can bring about a bout of lethargy that can knock you on your ass and leave you watching *Saved By the Bell* reruns for weeks. As the blood soaks into the compressed metal, the device will turn a dark shade of black. Once the entire object is black, rinse the shuriken with a garden hose. You should also dispose of the poke body by bringing it to the ancient poke burial grounds in Antarctica.

STEP SIX: Sharpen. Circular-saw-toothed salamanders are recommended.

STEP SEVEN: Throw at something you want to kill.

Opinjas: Pirates

They're dirty, poorly educated, disabled dolts who don't know booty from booty.

—Sir Shivilry, age 72

I would do Johnny Depp in a Chili-fest outhouse.

—Killisa, age 15

Great for trying out a new weapon. Nothing dies as fun as a pirate.

—Gaul McDartknee, age unknown

They're what you get when you breed a cockroach and a Catholic.

—Tomb Eyes, age 212

There really needs to be a set limit so that there are enough for everyone.

—Upper Hand, age 42

Sometimes I pretend like they might defeat me, just to listen to the funny way they talk for a while. It's a hoot.

—Green Night, age 21

What do you think?

_____

_____

Draw a picture of a pirate below and describe how you would kill him.

The Goldilocks Complex

If you signed up to be a ninja because you wanted fame, you should quit now and start designing video games. Much of what makes a ninja powerful is his or her ability *not* to be known. It is with this in mind that you must be warned about a syndrome that affects a lot of folks along the nonja path. The Goldilocks Complex. Ironically, the Goldilocks Complex is not very complex at all. It's quite simply the latent and involuntary desire to leave behind even the smallest bit of evidence to prove that you have been some place. It stems from a desire to get credit for what you're doing, even if the very thing you are doing is supposed to be sneaking into your sister's bedroom or your boss's office undetected. The following preventive steps will help eliminate the risk of contracting this deninjafying affliction.

1. *CSI*? Watch any Jerry Bruckheimer crime scene investigation show. One episode will do since they are all exactly the same. Now ask yourself honestly and with the intensity of David Caruso: Would the keen and smoldering veteran with personal demons have caught you? What about the entirely too sexy lab assistant? Perhaps the spicy Latina detective and the suspiciously in-shape computer expert working as a team? You have to be able to fool them all if you want to be a ninja.

2. "CATMANDER" AND CHIEF Paint an LOL cat on the forehead of the president of the United States using invisible ink. Your challenge is to leave without taking any of the supercool president stuff lying around. Not the ball of zimploraflax given as a peace offering from the Meluneegreefuths. Not the Air Force One

peanut M&M's. Not the briefcase labeled "The End." We are ninjas, not burglars. We must resist the impulse to "collect." It clutters your life and can become rather creepy if gone unchecked.

3. **FAT CRIB** Live for one month inside the blubber folds of a morbidly obese shut-in without their knowledge. You are not allowed to leave their body for any reason during the entire month, even if they die. You will be able to subsist upon the sweat, crumbs, and insects living within the folds.

4. **GATES KEEPER** Without his knowledge, replace Bill Gate's entire home and business computing setup with Apple products. If done correctly it should be a full 30 days before he gets his first iPhone bill and realizes the switch has occurred.

5. **THE BHARK TEST** This is the big one. Because they're a genetic combination of bears and sharks, bharks do have arguably one of the best senses of smell among aquatic furred mammals. Your challenge is to remove a baby bhark from his mother's marsupial pouch without her becoming aware of you. As an additional challenge, slice yourself open wrist to elbow on both arms before entering the ocean.

A bhark searches for seaquins.

WEAPON HIGHLIGHT
SWORD

Ever need to cut a throat? Open a back of a robotic tiger? Whittle a giant wooden stake, slice off a limb, or punch a hole in a basilisk? Want to metaphorically screw a pack of wolverines, make pig shavings to attract those wolverines, or trim the mouths of those wolverines as they are trying to bite you?

A good sword can help you with all of those tasks and millions more. A good sword for general use has a comfortable handle, a sturdy hilt, and a really really sharp blade that sticks outward.

Keep your fingers and the rest of your body clear of the sharp blade as you draw and sheath your sword.

Sword safely sheathed

Correct

Incorrect

SAFE SWORD USE

DO keep sword hidden except when you are using it, and even then you usually want to mask it as much as possible.

DO cut things that are not your body parts.

DO stab people who try and take your sword.

DO keep your sword sharp and clean. Just try facing down a Bipolar Bear with a dull blade.

DO obey any transmeditory laws of weaponry. Swords are not welcome on all planes of consciousness (e.g., Origamium).

DO NOT carry your sword whimsically or in staged musicals.

DO NOT throw your sword. You should have plenty of other sharp and deadly things to whip at people.

DO NOT stab, slice, or thrust toward yourself unless you are absolutely certain you can stop the sword before it stabs, slices, or thrusts you (demonized limbs are an exception).

DO NOT be hesitant about using your sword in con-junction with another weapon. If it is a proper ninja sword you should be able to attach chains and bull-whips for building up speed and reaching around cor-ners, bat shurikens, flip other ninjas, do anything your freaky mind can think of in the heat of battle.

I recall when I first started training in the sword I was concerned because my master didn't have a head. I thought his lack of eyes, ears, nose, mouth, and brain would limit his ability to teach. Boy, was I wrong. By the time I left him, I was seriously considering removing my own head in pursuit of his genius. If I didn't love lemon sorbet so much, I am confident I would have.

—Shank Yu Varimatch, ninja, sword master

SUGGESTED SWORD READING

The following compendiums not only contain many wonderfully fine points about sword use, but are also each written on one-of-a-kind swords.

Now You Don't See It, Now You're Dead, written by Lady Die on the Blade of Gory

Of Slice and Zen, written by The Lord of Swords on Swingy Todd

Through the Cutting Glass, written by Mark Pain on the Chevy Impaler

WARNING: Before weapon use, be sure to consult "Weapon Care and Training," page 275.

Certified Ninja Products for Beginners

Whether you're training at home or heading out on your first assassination, these items will help you live to tell about it. These and other deadly fine certified ninja products can be found in hidden authorized shops in most major malls. (See our full-page ads in *BruiseWeak* and *EnterPainment Sneakly.*)

Blackie's Bag of Pointy Things

Great for teaching you to fight in the moment, this potpourri bag of sharp objects is full of surprises. Each bag contains 24 random pointy things that can range from an extremely sharpened pencil to a bucktoothed cobra or the corner of a table.

Knife Monkey

One rabid rhesus monkey wearing a lightweight suit of razor-sharp switch-blades. Let this insane and armed primate loose in your home and get ready for hours of life-threatening fun.

Sand

An eight-ounce bag of grade-A multiuse sand. Comes with three 10,000-page manuals: *Sand Skills for Beginners*, *Beach of Death*, and *Grains of Annihilation*.

Weapon Trick Kit

Sure you have a bo staff, but can it twist apart in the middle to break into two halves connected by a chain? It could if it was tricked out with Whammy's Weapon Trick Kit. This 98-piece set of chains, fasteners, and ball bearings has everything you need to transform your boring sword into a boring sword, your nunchucks into an old knotty cane, your poison darts into fashionable earrings!

Flamco's Throwing Fire

A staple for any ninja. Each case contains 20 fire bursts (10 orange/10 white). Flamco's patented fire technology ensures a reliable and powerful disbursement of premium hot flame with each toss. (Blue, black, and clear fire also available; see our ad in *Boy's Death* magazine for more information.)

Grandma Knickerbottom's Eviscerators

Anyone who has tried to pull out the innards of a forked-tongue spitting walrus knows that eviscerating can be a messy job, cumbersome, and awkward. Let everyone's favorite grandma give you a hand . . . or rather a hook . . . with a saber attached to it! The Knickerbottom family has spent centuries developing and honing the perfect tools for slicing open bellies and getting all that stuff inside, out. So sharp and sturdy that even a grandma can use it, each eviscerator comes with four scrumptious recipes for turning those nasty vitals into yummy vittles.

The Bleeding Edge

Before attempting the next step on the path, take a few seconds to assess and confirm your worthiness.

MASTER'S WRAP-UP

Meet with a ninja master and discuss your progress. Spar with him in an open, dusty field with high winds. Attack him with all forms and weapons you know.

CLANVERSATIONS

Discuss the following questions with your clanmates.

1. What is life?

2. What is not life?

3. What is something each clan member could do to be seen less?

4. Who is the most likely member to betray the clan?

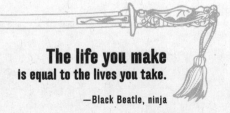

The life you make
is equal to the lives you take.

—Black Beatle, ninja

4

Ninjaish

The Ninja regales his apprentice with a fascinating story as they carefully hunt for demon elves.

We seem to lose the most people during this stage of the path. It seems like that primarily because it is where we lose the most people. In all honesty, we don't really lose them so much as they lose their lives or at least significant parts of their body. Some die due to lack of commitment. Some due to horrible beasts with pandimensional digestive tracts. Some due to not-so-horrible beasts with regular-old digestive tracts.

The point is, if you don't want to become someone who is dead, you will want to do a fair bit more than what you conceive is possible during this stage of the path.

For once there was a ninja who was turned into a mouse by a vitch* and thrown into a pit of hungry boa constrictors. It was most certainly to be his death. However, the doomed ninja mouse refused to accept only the logical possibilities of the situation. He produced a tiny little guitar case and opened it up. Dozens of beautiful dancing dolls jumped out, captivated the snakes, and draped ether-soaked clothes over their noses. When the boas awoke, they were on the moon with their bellies full of vitch au graten, and the mouse was on tour in Europe with a children's theatre show called Reason to be Fearful.

Ninjaish is also a special stage because much of its exploration and involvement takes place in the mind. It is sometimes called the "thinking chapter." Not by ninjas, but by stupid people who *think* there is a separation between body and mind. It will not surprise you that most of those people end up with their minds separated from their bodies . . . by a ninja.

* Vampiress/Witch/Friendless.

Ninjaish Requirements

As you battle for awesomeness in this chapter, you must also accomplish the requirements below, or so help us, you will not finish the chapter. And by finish, we mean live through.

After accomplishing each challenge, you must make a scroll describing your triumph. Then burn the scroll and eat the ashes (it is okay to mix with lemon ice if needed).

☐ **1.** Demonstrate how fire works, plays, and gets away from it all.

☐ **2.** Use the Ten Tools of Terror to scare something to death.

☐ **3.** Show what to do for surprise attacks

    a. On you

    b. On them

☐ **4.** Inflict unimaginable levels of pain on something that deserves it.

☐ **5.** Prepare and perform a two-act play with your clan that includes the following.

    a. Real suspense

    b. Believable characters (with believable motives)

    c. Compelling emotional depth

    d. Universal truth that is naturally and logically folded into the dramatic structure

    e. Satisfying resolution that is perfect, but not too perfect

    f. An amazing, kick-butt fight sequence

☐ **6.** Find the traces of lies and manipulation in everything you have ever heard.

☐ **7.** Participate in at least one mission that involves "bringing it."

☐ **8.** By yourself, create five life-threatening situations for unsuspecting adversaries.

☐ **9.** Don't stop.

☐ **10.** Remove all traces of your existence prior to beginning this book.

You Can't Spell Disguise Without a Gui

Your black gui is your second skin. It masks your first skin and anything that you can't hide on your first skin. Take pride in your gui and keep it in perfect order.

A true ninja gui is made from the skin of a flabricorn, an oversized, flabby, horned horse with no legs. It moves by sticking its horn in the ground for leverage and rolling. It is also the only animal with a durable, breathable epidermis that can withstand heat in excess of 4,000 degrees.

A flabricorn daydreams about deep-fried cheese dipped in caramel.

Flabricorn hide is a great material, but it's stark white when dried and prepared for sewing. A dye is needed. A black dye. A *real* black dye. All regular black dyes in the world are either really dark red, really dark green, or really really dark white. The only truly black thing in the world that can be used to dye ninja gui is blood from the heart of a demon dragon. A lot of dragon blood is black, but most of it is poisonous and therefore unusable. But demon dragons have to fly between life and death, and in order to do that, they have to have pure hearts (no poison). That works out well for the ninja.

What doesn't work out well for the ninja is the fact that demon dragons are huge, flying, fire-breathing lizards intent on devouring the souls of the living. They have eyes that can see directly into your truth and a tiny woman's mouth on the tip of their center arm that can emulate the exact vocal pattern of any mother, girlfriend, or porn star. This makes getting its heart very difficult. Difficult, but not impossible. (See *Dragon Demising,* by Clyde the Glide.)

Once the dragon is dead and your gui is dyed, you will begin to look like a real ninja, but no one will know that because real ninjas are really hard to see. Make sure to line the inside of your gui with lots of hidden pockets and pouches for storing cool ninja weapons and devices. Sew some oddly shaped compartments that don't fit anything you currently own. You'll find something dangerous to put in them soon enough.

One of the many challenges confronting the modern ninja is washing the gui. You should wash your gui after each use. This is why there are very few French ninjas. A Febreze or Drakkar once-over will not do. You need to give your ninja suit a real good scrubbing that gets out not only the blood and guts, but also any spells or curses that might have attached themselves to you during your mission.

Regular people don't recognize how vulnerable they are during laundering. You got the jangly quarters, the loud machines, and the creepy people talking to you who don't seem to be doing any laundry. That is why the first step in washing your gui is to steal a washing machine and transmi-

WARM-WEATHER CLOTHING CHECKLIST

☐ **Black gui covering 98 percent of your body**

COLD-WEATHER CLOTHING CHECKLIST

☐ **Black gui covering 99 percent of your body**

grate to the Cuddle Puppy Cloud Realm, which is the closest parallel plane with 2/20 power.

Now, although this place is safer than your home or local Laundromat, remember that the Cuddle Puppy Cloud Realm is full of C.U.D.D.L.E. Puppies. C.U.D.D.L.E. is, of course, an acronym for Certain Undeniable Death-Dealing Life-Eviscerating . . . Puppies. These adorable juvenile canines are 400 hundred feet tall, attracted to the smell of wet lint, and completely untrainable. If one of them decides to go to town on your leg, you will never walk again. It don't take a Russian dancer to tell you that you ain't got time for a spin cycle.

Making a Mission Plan

A mission plan prepares you for the challenges you expect to face when going to kill, spy on, or retrieve something from an enemy. No mission plan can prepare you for the unexpected because that doesn't make any sense, but a good mission plan will give you focus, perspective, and a good starting place for blame if everything goes to crap.

THE FOUR Ys

WHERE are you going to kill, spy on, or retrieve something?

WHEN are you going to kill, spy on, or retrieve something?

WHO are you going to kill, spy on, or retrieve something from?

WHY are you going to kill, spy on, or retrieve something from your who?

WHAT are you going to kill, spy on, or retrieve something from?

WASHING INSTRUCTIONS

Do not remove gui from body before washing.

Machine wash separately with invisible cranes.

Dry by jumping really fast into a demonimbus cloud.

HOW are you going to kill, spy on, or retrieve something from your who, during your when, at your where, using your what?

Upon a close examination you will notice that (1) there are more than four Ys, and (2) none of them begin with Y. You must be a ninja even when planning to be a ninja.

Missions are like snowflakes: every 4,768,235th one is exactly the same. That means most of them will be different. Even if a mission seems familiar, a responsible ninja looks closely for what might make it unique.

For once there was a very fine pants store that sold only the finest pants, trousers, and slacks. A very rich man walked into the store one day looking to replace his solid-gold jeans. The proprietor informed the man that they did not have exactly the same brand and cut in stock. The rich man scoffed, "The only thing that matters is that they're gold, you-not-as-wealthy idiot." The rich man snatched the first pair of gold jeans he saw, put them on, and paid the storeowner for them with his old gold pants and a diamond nose plug. Soon after leaving the shoppe, the rich man found himself being beaten savagely by a gang of gay werewolves. It was but an instant before his throat was torn out that the soon-to-be-dead, affluent, premier dungaree-donner heard one of the Pink Bears say, "That's what you get for wearing assless jeans when you have 'Oscar Wilde was trite!' tattooed on your ass." Because the depraved fat cat had failed to (1) wear underwear and (2) consider the exceptional attributes of his purchase, he had to be identified by his dental records.

Reaffirming the Code

A NINJA IS . . .	SPECIFIC EXAMPLE THAT PROVES THAT I AM LIVING BY THIS
Loyal	
Deadly	
Sneaky	
Death-dealing	
Flexible	
Deathly	
Clever	
Dangerous	
Focused	
Lethal	
Amazing	
Violent	
Hidden	
Slayish	
Cheerful	

Disorienteering

For thousands of years, man and beast have developed tools, instruments, and senses for finding their way. A sense of direction is the most securing factor for any living thing. Knowing where you are in relationship to stuff (or in a relationship for that matter) gives you confidence, calm, and control. A ninja can rob an adversary of that peace of mind using special disorienting methods.

SHADOW STICK METHOD

The forest is full of twigs, branches, and sticks. There's nothing special about them . . . unless they're attached to a ninja. The Shadow Stick Method aims to disorient a woodland traveler without him, her, or it having any knowledge of your presence.

Before you employ this method, you should know what you're trying to disorient. Not everything will disorient the same. Different things have different senses with different degrees of sensation. Most persons have between two and four eyes, almost always on the head and hands, while a Shoggoth has a myriad of eyes that constantly form and unform all over its body.

• Start by sneaking around the wooded area and gathering a healthy pile of sturdy sticks and twigs. Make sure you do this without the knowledge of the squirrels and birds. They can get possessive about their wood, and you don't want to start something that will end up with 50 cute woodland carcasses lying around. That is sure to arouse suspicion in your mark. Make sure you have gathered enough sticks to also cover your entire body.

• Spy on the thing you wish to disorient and strategically place the sticks in its path. The first stick is the most crucial. It needs to come out of nowhere and trip the mark. But not just any trip will do. You must trip him so that he falls in a specific way onto your other sticks.

• The other sticks should be braced at precise angles so that they jab into ALL of the ocular, aural, and nasal cavities of the mark. Make sure you get 'em all. If you miss an ear or an eye, he may not become disoriented or, worse yet, may get wise to your scheme.

• Position yourself (in your stick suit) so that as he reaches for something to pull him up, he finds a branch that just happens to be your arm. Just as he arrives at upright, make the sound of a branch breaking while quickly pulling your arm away from him.

• As he falls, use your leg, which will appear to be a branch, to guide his head toward the large stone that you have hidden under some twigs.

• Once the mark is unconscious, move him to an entirely different forest.

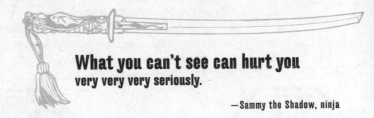

What you can't see can hurt you
very very very seriously.

—Sammy the Shadow, ninja

THE WATCH METHOD

Maps, compasses, and informative signs are the guidance tools of many. By watching what his mark is watching, a ninja can disorient him without ever touching him.

• **Map.** Steal the map of your mark the night before he departs. Produce an exact replica of the map with a few minor exceptions. Alter the course so that the destination appears to be one thing (e.g., Grandma's House) but is actually another (e.g., a Cave of Butter Scorpions). Place the altered map exactly where you found the real map. In the morning, sit back and watch your mark confidently stride toward death with his "trusty" map.

• **Compass.** Catch a bugbear (every woods/jungle has one or two). Feed him a nice big dinner of great green globs of greasy grimy gopher guts and high-powered magnets. At sunrise, as your mark sets out, release your bugbear with a belly full of intense polarized metal. As the bugbear moves in giant circles without being seen—as is its nature—watch as your mark conscientiously follows his compass around and around. If your mark is ambitious enough to actually catch up with the Bugbear, then you've got the special treat of front row seats to the dead show.

• **Signs.** Horrible movie, great disorienter. Every ninja loves marks who watch road signs. They are like silly little lambs that can read. For this technique, all you have to do is travel one sign ahead of your mark and secretly mess with each sign in a clever way. As this technique has seen common usage in animated programming and old Herbie movies, I.O.N. suggest that you carefully consider your sign altering so as to not alert your mark.

Original.

Bad alteration. No one except a Scotsman or a werewolf would be dumb enough to fall for this.

Original.

Good alteration.

WATCH FOR FALLING ROCKS

Original.

STAND HERE FOR A WHILE... AND POOP

Bad alteration. It started out okay, but really got greedy at the end.

BERLIN   500km

Original.

WELCOME TO BERLIN

Good alteration. You have simply convinced your mark that he has already arrived at his destination.

THE CONSTELLATION METHOD

The stars have been a popular and reliable tool for navigation throughout the ages. As a ninja, knowing this can help you to misdirect people trying to find their way at night. This is basically the old-school version of sign changing: star changing.

As you may know, constellations are groupings of stars that are most visible at night and seem to form some sort of vague representation of something. A crab or a belt or a dipper. Even the most accomplished astronomers and ship captains can never recall exactly what the celestial objects are supposed to look like.

All that a good ninja needs to do to set a traveler off course is bound along in the trees or clouds above your mark cleverly shooting hang fire* in

---

* Stone-sized white floating flames from the sweet old country where I come from, where nobody works and nothing ever gets done.

calculated positions to create the illusion of alternate constellations. Below are a few examples.

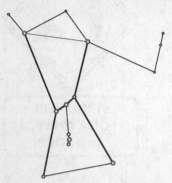

a. It doesn't take much to turn Orion into the Pisces.

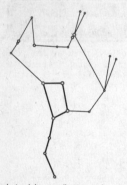

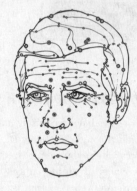

b. Look how easily Ursa Major can be converted into Lee Majors.

c. The North Star changes into the "Hang in There" kitten in an instant (and that's not even a real constellation).

THE OLD REDIRECT

This is a rarely used method, but a good one to know if your mark is stupid enough to be using a GPS system. Simply hack into the navigational program they are using and rewrite the algorithm from "shortest possible route" to "most round-about-and-ass-backward route possible."

Example:

YAHOOGLE MAP

Start:	1600 Pennsylvania Avenue NW, Washington, DC 20006
End:	1060 W. Addison, Chicago, IL 60613
Travel:	705 miles—about 6 hours 29 minutes (up to 7 hours in traffic)

1.	GO TO WASHINGTON/DULLES INTERNATIONAL AIRPORT	27.5 MILES
2.	FLY TO CHICAGO (ORD)	666.7 MILES
3.	CATCH A CAB TO WRIGLEY FIELD	13.8 MILES

These directions are for planning purposes only. You may find that construction projects, traffic, or other events may cause road conditions to differ from the map results.

FACTS OF DEATH

Ninjas do not approve of regular homosapien astrological charting. This is due primarily to the fact that ninjas have battled and defeated all of the represented creatures and understand their universal truth in relation to life. The ninja instead uses an Astrological Chart made up of signs defined by the space *around* the stars rather than the stars themselves. 36,500 black forms make up the Ninjastrological Chart.

YAHOOGLE MAP

Start: 1600 Pennsylvania Avenue NW, Washington, DC 20006

End: 1060 W. Addison, Chicago, IL 60613

Travel: 7,000,005 miles—about 11 years 29 minutes (up to 12 years in traffic)

1.	GO TO LINCOLN BEDROOM. REMOVE PICTURE OF MARY TODD.	73 FEET
2.	CUT MOUTH OUT OF PICTURE, PROCEED TO FRONT GATE AND TALK TO GUARDS THROUGH THE PICTURE'S MOUTH HOLE.	.1 MILE
3.	BUY CRAPPY CAR FROM ONE OF THE GUARDS AND PAY HIM IN SPIT.	.1 LOVE
4.	STOP BY BEN'S CHILI BOWL FOR A HALF-SMOKE AND SOME "WORKS" FRIES.	ON THE WAY
4.	DRIVE TO KRAZY KEN'S KOSTUMES. ACQUIRE AND PUT ON AN AUTHENTIC BORG COSTUME.	4.5 MILES
5.	BOARD A TRANSPORT FOR CAPRICA.	700 FEET (DOWN)
6.	TURN RIGHT INTO AN OLD FRIEND FROM COLLEGE.	2 INCHES
7.	HEAD TO THE MOS EISLEY CANTINA TO CATCH UP OVER A FEW PINTS OF ROMULAN ALE.	5 AIRLOCK CHECKPOINTS
8.	KEEP ON, KEEP ON, KEEP ON, KEEP ON DANCING.	ALL THROUGH THE NIGHT
9.	WAKE UP IN MYANMAR (FORMERLY BURMA) NEXT TO A HAM ON RYE (FORMALLY, A PIG AND A TALL GRAIN GRASS).	UNKNOWN
10.	GO STRAIGHT INTO A TRAINING MONTAGE.	THE DISTANCE
11.	TURN LEFTIST.	10%
12.	CONTINUE TALKING ABOUT PROBLEMS AND NOT DOING ANYTHING ABOUT THEM.	1 MILE/MINUTE
13.	FIND PURPOSE.	IN SOUL (NOT IN SEOUL)
14.	FOLLOW YOUR DREAMS.	WHEREVER
15.	GO NOWHERE.	.0 MILES
16.	TURN RIGHT WHERE YOU STARTED.	.0 MILES
17.	TURN RIGHT UP YOUR ALLEY.	10

18.	GO FOR IT.	4 ITS
19.	GET INTO SOME "BAD STUFF."	6 KILOS
20.	ENTER REHAB.	12 STEPS
21.	FIND YOURSELF AT DINNER WITH JUDGMENTAL FAMILY MEMBERS.	ETERNITY
22.	GO TOO FAR.	2 FARS
23.	GO DOWN EASY.	1'S PRIDE
24.	DIVE INTO A RELATIONSHIP HEADFIRST.	DEEP
25.	BE THERE.	4 HER
26.	GET LEFT.	A SAD MOMENT
27.	STAY THE COURSE.	TOO LONG
28.	TURN INTO YOUR PARENTS.	OVERNIGHT
29.	GO UNDER THE KNIFE.	$5,000 DEDUCTIBLE
30.	HEAD DIRECTLY INTO THE LIGHT.	6 FEET UNDER

These directions are for planning your demise only. You may find that destruction projects, horrible accidents, or other life events may cause unlivable conditions that differ from the map results.

Where Are You Going?

Remember, any tool that you can use against an enemy may also be used against you. Therefore, it is highly recommended that you build a disorienteering course with your clan to practice keeping your wits about you when something is trying to set you off course.

Ninjas train on special courses that really mess with their perception of space, but that doesn't mean you can't make your own mini gauntlet to increase your skills in your own backyard.

STEP ONE: Stick six wooden posts and dozens of long, pointy objects into the lawn with the sharp part sticking up.

STEP TWO: Fill your backyard with boiling tar mixed with Compound 1080. Make sure all of the sharp things and the posts are sticking out above the tar and concentrated cellular metabolism blocker.

STEP THREE: Knock out the power grid in your area and wait for the dark of night.

STEP FOUR: Hold a baseball bat to your forehead with the other end touching the ground and spin around 100 times as fast as you can.

STEP FIVE: Now jump from post to post through the yard while your clanmates whip bricks and Molotov cocktails at you.

Make sure everyone gets a turn and keep track of your times. Many dens use this as a warm-up bonding exercise before heading out for a mission.

The Art of Bull

If you're reading this, you're amazing. I mean that. No, not everybody who's reading this. Just *you*. The way your eyes scan the page. Oh, man, I bet those eyes get you out of all sorts of trouble . . . or into it. Ha ha ha. I don't know what it is, but you have this quality about you. I've never met anyone who can simultaneously make me feel skintinglingly excited and completely at ease. You're one of a kind. Someone should write a book about you. It would sell more copies in a week than all of those Harry Potter books combined. You're everything I want to be when I grow up. And that T-shirt makes you look like Josh Hartnett.

Gotcha, didn't we? That was flattery.

As you will learn in the next chapter, the ninja needs to be a master of sound. One of the greatest things you can do with sound is to flatter. Flattery will not get you everywhere, but it can usually get you close enough to inflict a deadly strike.

Flattery does not merely consist of compliments and exaggerated falsehoods. It is an art. The art of making someone feel more important and better than they actually are. You can imagine how that overconfidence can assist a warrior.

Yet flattery used incorrectly can be a poison toothpick in the mouth of success. Bad flattery can embolden and bolster an enemy and aid them in finding untapped reserves of endurance and strength to fight back. You need to learn the difference and just how fine the line is between a complimentary sentence and a death sentence.

DEVICES OF FLATTERY

NO, YOU! (Compliment of Darkness)
The ninja have a long and unwritten history of being able to disarm an opponent and then immediately

use that disarmed weapon masterfully against the opponent it was just taken from. It is little wonder that ninjas have devised a similar technique for complimentary combat.

No, You! is a specialized device developed by Master O'Stop. It involves taking a compliment that was just given to you, amplifying it, and sending it back with rock guitar force at the complimenter.

Here's an example.

COMPLIMENTER: Wow! You're really fast.
NINJA: No. You're so much faster. So blindingly fast, in fact, that light is jealous.

While the complimenter bathes in the buttery glow of the ninja's blarney, the ninja has thrown a ciriken* at the complimenter's heart.

YOU CAN, TOO (Shadow Massage)
A ninja trains in so many techniques that at least one of them is bound to impress or intrigue almost any foe you face. Although it may have taken you hundreds of painful hours to master a skill, your complimenter doesn't know that. This provides a powerful tool that should not be overlooked.

You Can, Too is the art of convincing an awkward amateur to try a tremendously difficult, advanced ninja skill. The goal, of course, is getting someone to basically inflict great harm or death upon himself.

Example: Your opponent has heard that you can jump off a cliff and quickly grab one blade of grass to keep from falling (Superlite's Method).

NINJA: "Sure. That's really really easy. All you have to do is think about an Air Supply song. There's a cliff. You should try it. It's so easy. It's certainly not like you have to build a transcendental avatar of yourself and replace your mass with its electronic code in a split second."

* A circular shuriken with many teeth and a hollow center. Often called a "sawblade shuriken." When thrown correctly, it can burrow 10 to 12 centimeters into bone and flesh.

If executed correctly the next sound your opponent makes will be SPLATT!

It is also often assumed that a ninja can do many things that they cannot. You can use the You Can, Too device for these situations as well. Remember, what they don't know can only hurt them.

Example: You opponent has heard that ninjas can blow themselves up with C4 and reassemble their bodies using meditation.*

NINJA: "Yep. Absolutely. Did it twice this morning. It's a great party
          trick. Here's some C4 and a handheld detonator. Give it a try. It'll
          be great. I'll just be over here behind this metal wall a hundred
          meters away."

BOOM! SPLATT!

YOU ROCK! (Super Spin Hook)
This is one technique you don't want to try unless you are very good at lying. This device is a hardcore, endless barrage of adulation. Bombarding an opponent with so much bootlicking, brownnosing, and beslavering that their ego quite literally explodes.

Example: Let's say you're facing down an Azhi Dahaka.† Well, no matter how much you train, no single ninja is taking down that three-headed dragon in a physical fight. It has a thousand senses. Pretty tough to get a drop on something that can perceive the emotions of atoms. Not to mention, if you cut one, it bleeds snakes and scorpions. Who's gonna be worse off from that wound? Your only option is flattery.

NINJA: "Man, look at you. You are striking and formidable. I can't believe
          I'm standing in your presence. Your skin is amazing. It's like the
          color of awesome. And those eyes. I'm having a hard time deciding

* Someday this may be achieved, but currently ninjas can only do this with odd-numbered Cs.
† An obnoxious, red, snakelike dragon who drives a flying Mercedes.

which of the six of them to gaze into longingly. Is that a new tie?
It goes perfectly with your wings of ice. You make Ryan Seacrest
look like a barf-covered turd. But not one of your turds, of course.
I see one of your beautiful poops over there. Damn, even your
turds are spectacular. Fabulous job. You're like the best thing ever
wrapped up in whatever the thing is that would eventually outbest
that thing. That's right, Dr. Bitchin', you're future-best. I'm trying to think up new words just to tell you how breathtaking your
spine-horn is. Magwonderawejestic! You on a T-shirt would unite
the world. You smell like elegance and power dipped in far-out.
When I was growing up, I used to dress up like you every day. I
can only perform sexually by imagining that I am you having rela-
tions with another you. The way your tails move reminds me of a
thousand Justin Timberlakes. I wish I had two mouths like you
do so that I could talk about you more. Your breathing has become
my religion. I am working on a 400-part documentary about you
called *AWESOME!* Staring at you is like physically being in a
dream that's receiving oral sex from chocolate. Briltastical. That's
another new word inspired by your indefinable perfection. Anyone
who considers themselves a god is no more than one molecule of
your eye vomit. You are the future of art. I believe the Internet will
eventually evolve into just you on every page and everyone in the
world will dedicate their lives to playing a MMORPG about you
and all the phenomenal stuff that you do all the time. The game
will be called Universe of the Major-League Fablorious Mostest.
I know my brain is nothing compared to your cerebral splendor,
but right and wrong don't make sense when I look at your fault-
lessness. I have officially filled out the paperwork to change my
name to Wishiwasyou. I love Target and own lots of stock in the
company, but if someone made a doll of you and they didn't sell it
there, I would figure out a way to destroy the entire corporation.
I could express my love for you so much better if every word in
every language was replaced with your name. I just lost control
of my bodily functions thinking about your bodily functions. You
are Suparagonellent multiplied by Transquisitepitome. Existence
is jealous of you. You're simply the best. Better than all the rest.
You're the best around. Nothing's ever gonna keep ya down. You
make my dreams come true. I love you, I honestly love you. You're
fast machine, you keep your motor clean, you're the best damn
dragon that I've ever seen. You you you make a grown man cry, you

you make a dead man come. You're the one that I want. Let's get it on. Thank you for giving me the best day of my life. You're the first, my last, my everything. Nothing compares to you. You look wonderful tonight. I want you to want me. I would die for you. It's a little bit funny this feeling inside. You make my heart sing. Every little thing you do is magic. You're three times a lady. I would do anything for love and I WILL do that. How do I live if living is without you. Baby, I love your way. You're unforgettable and always on my mind. I'll stop the world and melt with you. You rock me like a hurricane. You are the first creature to ever truly make me wave my hands in the air and wave them like I just don't care."

KABOOM!

I bet you'd be great at practicing your flattery.

Gotcha again, didn't we? We don't know you. This is a book. But you fell for it because we were earnest and looked you straight in the eye. Ninety percent of flattery is lying. Practice your flattery. Spend one month BSing everyone. Compliment constantly, but make sure each acclamation is perceived as genuine. Look into people's eyes. Rub their hands. Each time you see them, shake your head in disbelief as if you're waking from a dream. Challenge yourself by getting in trouble and then flattering your way out of it.

Suggestions: Kick a judge in the balls, call a karkadann* a rhinoceros, pee on the magazine shelf at your local library.

Poisonous Beast Jumble

Unscramble the following word jumbles to make the names of the beasts pictured above.

* A rather rhinoceros-looking creature.

G-O-D

T-I-G-E-R-H-A-W-K-O-C-T-O-P-U-S

A-E-I-I-K-M-M-N-P-P-P-R-U-V

_____

H-H-H-H-H-H-H-H-H

_____

Catch a Phrase and You're Killing on Top of the World

By now, you are pretty good at killing. It's time to start adding some flair. Now, it's important to note that this is not Terrell Owens–style flair that ostracizes the rest of the team and breeds resentment so that no matter how much natural talent and depth they have, they can't even pull off a division win. Nor is it the type of flair that an Applebee's employee reluctantly wears to present a false image of wackiness in hopes of making you buy more grease and overdramatically named daiquiris. Ninja flair is made up of cool things that increase the general awesomeness of shadow warriors.

A catchphrase can be a powerful piece of flair.

"That's what she said."

"Not today."

"You're a _____."

These are all classic catchphrases started by ninjas. They are glorious, flexible, and commanding. Like a ninja.

You should have one.

Use the following worksheet to help you develop your catchphrase. Remember, all official catchphrases must be approved by the International Order of Ninjas before professional use.

1. **WARM UP** by trying to add the most potent and wicked words into the following phrases.

> a. You have the _____ of a _____.
>
> b. Really? I thought that your middle name was _____.
>
> c. I can _____ _____s with my eyes shut.
>
> d. Rock 'n' roll is dead, and I'm the _____ that _____ it's _____.
>
> e. Damn. That move was _____.

2. **FOR THIS EXERCISE,** pack your entire personality in the following words as you pronounce them. It may be helpful to surround yourself with hungry hungry hippos to keep you focused.

- Really
- What
- Unh
- Hooahh
- Understandable
- Yeah
- Macaroni
- Okay
- Trippy
- Go

3. **WHAT IS YOUR BODY** going to be doing while you're saying your catchphrase? You'd better know. Arthur "Fonzie" Fonzarelli was known for his catchphrase "Aaaayy!" He would have looked pretty stupid saying it though, if it weren't accompanied with a pounding of his fist that made a car start or jukebox play or banner unfurl.

Insert your favorite body movements into the following descriptive sentences and then practice the motions.

a. I turn my _____ while my _____ goes up and down.

b. I grab my _____.

c. I _____ my _____ so that it makes
a _____ing sound.

d. I roll my _____ and lick my _____.

e. I light a _____ on fire.

4.   **WRITE DOWN 10** embarrassing facts about yourself and give them to 10 obnoxious and indiscreet people. How does their ensuing behavior make you feel? What do you wish you could say to your buddy while the two of you are standing over their lifeless bodies?

1. _____
2. _____
3. _____
4. _____
5. _____
6. _____
7. _____
8. _____
9. _____
10. _____

5. **MIX AND MATCH** one element from column A
    and one element from column B to help you
    decide what style of catchphrase you want.
    Notice that there are a few blank spaces at
    the bottom to add your own ideas.

COLUMN A
Holy
For the love of
What the
Shove it in your
Great
Julie Andrews
By the staff of
Cool
Run for the
Well slap my
Blood-soaked
Jumpin'
I guess we're airing out our
Oooh!
And a healthy scoop of
Sexy, wet
Underwater
Let's eat
Yummy
Fucking

COLUMN B
Puppies
Texas
Fatty Arbuckle
Luggage
Mountains
Crack den
Kissinger
Casserole
Kitchen
Plumbers
Kazoos
Moses
Ass
Star Trek
Tiger Woods
Black hole
Nanny
Prince
Lips
Reality

WEAPON HIGHLIGHT
BO STAFF

Anything you've ever dreamed of doing with a stick you can do with a bo staff. In fact, when you strip away all of the bells and whistles, that's basically what a bo staff is—it's a stick. Sticks are an ancient weapon that date back to the time before ninjas. Scientinjas theorize that the very first ninja kill may have been with a stick (only later to be called a bo staff). That is why the sticks (bo staffs) used by ninjas are respected by fighters, foes, and fiends around the world.

Very basic bo staff.

Very fancy bo staff.

Although the basic shape (stick-shaped) remains the same, bo staffs come in many styles, ranging from light to heavy, rigid to flexible, and short to long. The shortest recorded bo staff was a one-centimeter-long mini toothpick wielded by the minja* War Whack Davis. He killed a giant with it by jumping down his throat and starting a mini tornado in his lungs. The longest recorded bo staff was a 239-foot tree trunk handled by Black Juice.

* A mini-ninja.

He also started a tornado with his bo staff, but it was a regular-sized one and was used to gather up a coven of banshees who had taken all of the soul out of Motown.

Although there is no blade attached to a traditional bo staff, it is still considered one of the most deadly and essential ninja weapons.

SAFE BO STAFF USE

DO swing it around as much as possible.

DO hit things repeatedly. Sometimes if the skin doesn't break, it's hard to tell how much damage you've really done. Keep wailing until you're sure.

DO pretend like it's a harmless walking stick that you need for your "bad leg" (wink).

DO protect your bo with a good water seal.

DO customize it with your "personality," but make sure it's stuff you're gonna be into for a while.

DO carry extra weapons just in case a stick isn't the solution to all your problems.

DO NOT use as a bindle pole or a water-carrying post. It's a weapon.

DO NOT write reminder notes on it or use it as your social calendar. It's a weapon.

DO NOT play stickball with it. It's a weapon.

DO NOT use your bo staff to fight things that breathe fire unless it is metal or bone or you are 100 percent sure your antiblaze enchantment is up to date.

DO NOT hesitate to hollow out a little hole on one end. Then you can put a dart or some acid in it. Your opponent will think, "Hey, he's just got that stick." FLICK! Acid face!

A bo staff is not a bat.

WARNING: Before weapon use, be sure to consult "Weapon Care and Training," page 275.

I started out as a shuriken thrower.
Some say I was the best they'd ever seen. That is until I was turned into a tree by a witch named the Barbed Bird. After about 20 years, the tree was struck by lightning, which turned all of me back into a real ninja, except for about five pounds around the middle that I'd been trying to lose anyway. Those five pounds that remained wood were in the shape of a six-foot stick. I named it Wonder Bo. Although I still get pains around the midsection when I swing it, I'll never use another weapon for the rest of my life.

—Roy the Hobbler, ninja

Opinjas: Guns

If you have to use a gun, you don't really know who you're killing.

—Bing Kilsby, age 350

Did you know that guns spelled backward is snug? Think about it. Right?

—Dier Maker, age 39

So sad. It's a gateway weapon that leads to laziness. Before you know it, everyone will be sitting in a bunker watching Fox News with their finger on a nuclear missile launcher.

—Stone, age 863

When I was 19, I did a guy in Laos from a thousand yards out. Rifle shot in high wind. Eight, maybe ten guys in the world could've made that shot.

—Lethal Weapon, age 52

If you play your cards right I just might give you a couple tickets to the show.

—Barry the Blade, age 27

Fun. Fun. Bang. Bang.

—Lucky Tiger, age 3

What do you think?

_____

_____

The Bleeding Edge

Before attempting the next step on the path, take a few seconds to assess and confirm your worthiness.

MASTER'S WRAP-UP

Meet with a ninja master and discuss your progress. Give him a scroll that lists everything you have killed. If he laughs, you are on the right track. If he breaks your arm, you may need to repeat this portion of the path.

CLANVERSATIONS

Discuss the following questions with your clanmates.

1. Wasn't that thing with the thing totally awesome?

2. How is my ninja training affecting my "mac" or "game"?

3. Who's your daddy?

NINJA PROVERB

One ninja makes a majority.

—Thorn Bird, ninja

Ninjalike

The Ninja and his apprentice agitate a pair of pain vipers before placing them in the bed of a really really really bad sixth-grader.

You have finally distinguished yourself from most humans, but just barely. You're showing mild signs of being someone who's interested in more than just wishing they were a ninja. You're ninjaish.

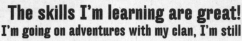

The skills I'm learning are great!
I'm going on adventures with my clan, I'm still alive and—*

—Michael J. O'Hara

Have a party, but make it a short hidden one that involves no sound or movement. The path has merely begun. You're doing it. Don't stop now.

Unless, of course, you're too afraid to continue.

In that case, stop. By all means stop. Go home. Sit on your couch, forget everything you have done to become ninjaish, and wait for patheticness to come and swallow you once again.

No?

All right. Then it's time to move forward. Another step. Another leap. Another potential incineration. The next step on your journey is to become ninjalike. If you look carefully at that word, your developing ninja senses will show you that it actually consists of two words: *ninja* and *like*. The meaning of the two words when combined is literally "like a ninja." That is a much more concrete association with ninjahood than your current rank of ninjaish. Holding the ninjalike rank is like going to the same school as Rupert Grint, the actor who plays Ron in the Harry Potter movies: You're close enough to see what it's like to be the man, but you're still far enough away to not have a real clue.

Your first question should be "How do I attain the rank of ninjalike without dying?"

Well, the bad news for 98 percent of you reading this is . . . you don't.

---

* His legs were bitten off at the hip by a gryphon before he could finish his sentence. A warning to future ninjas who think about wasting time and letting down their guard to reflect on an incomplete journey.

But if you've gotten this far, just keep on doing what you've been doing. Be quick, be alert, and just *be*. The path to becoming ninjalike is very much like having one of your teeth replaced with Joss Stone: painful and very annoying. To finish this chapter, it'll take the patience of a Spanish coin, and if you want to know what that really means, be patient.

In order to develop into being ninjalike, you must explore and master the five main senses of man: Sound, Sight, Smaste, Nerve, and Awareness. You must also learn the value of solitude and darkness and how to whittle in each.

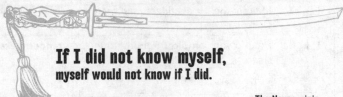

If I did not know myself,
myself would not know if I did.

—The Never, ninja

Ninjalike Requirements

As you battle for awesomeness in this chapter, you must also accomplish the requirements below, or so help us, you will not finish the chapter. And by finish, we mean survive.

After accomplishing each challenge, you must make a scroll describing your triumph. Then burn the scroll and eat the ashes (it is okay to mix with the Sigma Kappa sorority if needed).

☐ **1.** Master all the senses of man to a degree that would impress a real Las Vegas magician.

☐ **2.** Spend at least three months detached from your own consciousness.

☐ **3.** Fashion weapons for killing at least five Ninja Eaters using only things found in a video arcade.

☐ **4.** Plan meals for an overnight mission that do not require physically eating food, but still provide warrior-level nourishment.

☐ **5.** Complete the Physiomotional Confusion Checklist.

☐ **6.** Interview two respected people in your community and write an essay about how they are feeble and dysfunctional compared to a ninja.

☐ **7.** Identify the 10 deadliest inanimate objects in your school or workplace.

☐ **8.** Expand your physical training to include randomness and sleep.

a. Build a dream gauntlet.

b. Fight a creature that at least 90 percent of non-ninjas believe to be mythical or extinct.

c. Surprise yourself.

☐ **9.** Discuss with a master ninja when you should and should not be seen.

☐ **10.** Drop, jump, roll, flip, spin, turn, and slide into a void.

The Sound of Sound

A very common misconception about ninjas is that we never make any sound. Nothing could be closer to the truth but still miss the point entirely. Sound is a choice. A ninja decides not only on his sounds, but on many of his surrounding noises as well. In order to make sound a decision, you must understand how to make *no* sound and *all* sound.

YOUR SOUND

Everything you do makes a sound.

Walking to the courthouse.

Talking to a chicken about a girl you're too chicken to talk to.

Jumping through a spirit realm portal.

Operating the ventricles of your heart.

Thinking about the abundant and ever-changing classifications of celebrity.

They all make sounds. Master your sounds or perish at the hands and teeth of those who hear you.

SOUNDS I MAKE	
STEP 1:	Stand naked in the middle of a soundproof room and make all of the sounds your body can make. Make a mental (not physical) list of these sounds and store it in the lower left portion of your temporal lobe, keeping in mind that the very act of making a mental list makes a sound. While producing all your mouth and breath sounds, try singing the song "Take On Me" by a-ha as a shortcut. If sung correctly it will cover 89.5 percent of possible human vocal sounds. Remember, there are vast variations of burps and farts and that both sides of your face do not sound the same when slapped.
STEP 2:	Put on one or more layers of clothing and visit at least five of your most common destinations. Repeat as many of the sounds as possible in those locations. (Do not plan on making it through the entire a-ha song without being attacked.)
STEP 3:	Buy (do not rent) a pain viper from an I.O.N.-authorized wizard. Drink the appropriate amount of snake fury (one ounce for each pound of nerves) and agitate the pain viper with a hot poker or gossip about a distant family member. Then carefully apply viper to your genitals. The bite of the pain viper on your tenderest parts will cause you to make sounds you thought impossible for a human, screams and expressions no person could voluntarily produce. Note them. It is best if you are also naked for this step.

Now that you know what sounds you can make, what about the rest of the world? It would be ridiculous to think that one could know the full spectrum of the possible sounds of existence. Hearing wonderful new sounds of struggle and pain is part of the amazingly deadly journey of life. However, you can master the unknown by preparing yourself in the four major categories of sound.

MASTERING THE TYPES OF SOUND	
LOUD	The most natural reaction to a loud noise is to cover your ears. To the ninja, that makes about as much sense as ordering a P.B.J. sandwich with the peanut butter and jelly on the outside. If you want the sandwich that way, make it yourself. Not only is the volume of a sound a great factor for helping you analyze your foe, but covering your ears often takes one or more hands. Let's not be stupid, shall we? Loudness is a tool for the smart ninja and a weapon for the even-smarter ninja. Imagine a gryphat,* roaring as he flies in to eat your head. Simply hide in the waves of the sound until you can determine from which direction the urban winged lion is attacking, then you can get close enough to burn off his bewitched business-in-front/party-in-back mane. That loud sound just saved your life. A good mantra for loudness can be found in the lyrics of Paul Simon: "Shut the hell up, white fro." It was an unpublished song, but the former senator did write it . . . and it works. Shut up and attend some loud events. Go to a concert of a band with a bad pun name (e.g., Won Nothing Under Dog, Piece B With U). Can you kill them all before anyone realizes it's not part of the song? Spend a few days at Mardi Foie Gras (a.k.a. Zombie Geese Gone Wild). Can you snag 100 livers before they make you no longer a liver?

SOFT	Sure, ninjas are quiet. But just how quiet?
	  As quiet as a flea thinking about spitting on silk?
	  Quieter.
	  You must learn to be quieter than bug thoughts. Brain activity makes noise, along with most bodily functions, such as heart beating, lungs breathing, producing bile in the spleen, blinking your eyes, growing hair, etc. Mastering soft sounds means getting yourself to the point where you're making approximately as much sound as the idea of no sound. Then you can really begin to hear what's going on and what's not going on.
	
	  The best practice for soft sounds is death. Death is one of, if not, the quietest things in the world. Kill something and then listen to it. Although the material of the body may be making sounds, the life is not. That is death. The absence of life. Now, you can't be as quiet as death without dying, so don't do that, but being deathly quiet is a sure undetectable sign of a ninja.

* A gryphon with a mullet.

MASTERING THE TYPES OF SOUND	
"NORMAL"	Let us never forget that what is a normal sound for one creature can cause another's head to explode. Put together a fabulous disguise kit and go out into the world. Live among various creatures and cultures. Listen to their lives and to what they find normal. Did you know that the word *hamburger* means "sign up now and get a free gift" in mereese? How about that the sound of nails down a chalkboard is "aloha" to a squnk?* That all you need to kill a furisdiction† is the sound of an open carbonated beverage?
WEIRD	If you hear something and you don't know what it is, that's weird. Even if it just turns out that your cat has learned how to operate your Karaoke Revolution unit, it's still weird: A weird sound is a weird sound, even after you figure it out. As you've seen in many, many horrible horror movies, weird sounds can kill. You really need to manage your weird sounds and keep the list as small as possible. Make a list of everything that you think is weird. Then, using meditation, YouTube, and anime, gradually adjust your perceptions of the world until almost nothing seems odd, offensive, or vomitous.

Right Sight

Many practitioners of kung fu will argue that you cannot be a master unless you are blind. Practitioners of kung fu are kung fused.‡

But this book isn't about disparaging these complete imbeciles; it's about aligning your self with supremacy. In order to do that, you must be willing to see the world not only for what it is, but also for what it could be, should be, and isn't. Don't expect to become a master of the pandimensional inverse totality of darkness on day one. That's day two.

Here's the five-day path to mastering sight.

---

* Half squid/half skunk, all rebel. Shoots "stink ink" and doesn't give a crap what you think about his hair.
† Rage incarnate that is isolated to a specific area. It dines primarily on the ignorance of youth groups and gun clubs.
‡ Dad joke.

DAY ONE	Wake up, but don't open your eyes. In the black of your criminally messy, IKEA-laden, funky-smelling room, meditate into the void of perception. Adjust your visual spectrum to include everything. Then open your eyes, eat a good, well-balanced breakfast, and see everything.
DAY TWO	Now *really* see everything with the additional point of view of having already seen it before. Look at the things you pretended to see but didn't really. Look at them! Ninjas do not turn away. *The ogre turned the beautiful princess inside out and scraped the gooey insides from her bones as if she were a tremendously bloody artichoke. He then stripped bare and danced with wretched eroticism to the complete works of Devo played in reverse, while smearing himself with mastodon excrement. —from* 73 Real Tales for Little Ninjas, *by Undork Eviserstein*
DAY THREE	See the world for the first time. You may need to borrow the eyes of a small child or squirrel to really accomplish this. It is very important on this day that you do not stop seeing to sit down in a coffee shop or poorly named public park and start writing flowery poetry. Nothing narrows your ability to see like the phrase "golden fairies of light dancing on the skin of mother's bosom." Wording like that can set you back a full day in your goal of seeing. Seeing the world for the first time should be like learning to ride a flying porcupine: painful, surprising, and scary as bad French toast.
DAY FOUR	Visualize *It*. If you're not sure what "*It*" is, you're on the right path. Keep looking. *It* is a tremendously important element of essence. *It* is the stuff old movie producers and British elocutionists used to philosophize about. Did you ever wonder how an incredibly mediocre, half-talent like J-Lo could become a household name? It was *It*. She obviously slept with someone who had a lot of *It* and some of that person's *It* rubbed off on her . . . mostly in the rearish area. If it were not for the *It* she stole, Jennifer Lopez would still be on the block with at least one illegal substance in the pockets of her XXL sweat suit. Being able to see *It* is very important. There is only so much *It* in the world, and terrible things happen when *It* falls into the wrong hands (see *An Unfinished Life*).
DAY FIVE	Listen to Peter Gabriel's "In Your Eyes" enough. How much is enough? If you're becoming Ninjalike, you will know. If not, you will rather quickly descend into madness and begin worshipping a monkey named Sledgehammer.

After the fifth day, you are going to want to put your skills to the test. This is a good time to earn your Stone Sight merit brand. Start by tracking down a gorgoyle* and challenging her to a staring contest. Gorgoyles are already made of stone,

* Gorgon gargoyle.

A gorgoyle spies a discarded stick of lip balm.

so there is no mirror trickery to be pulled here. You have to instantaneously hypnotize the winged, snake-haired temptress while metaphysically stealing her essence and channeling it through your eyes. If she turns to fire, you've accomplished your goal. If you turn to stone, you're dead.

Smaste Schmaste

Everyone who has been to Texas or Wal-Mart knows that the ability to smell and the ability to taste are inextricably linked. Similarly, most alive people know that olfactory processes form the strongest link to memory.

The amazingness that a ninja becomes aware of is that taste forms an incredibly strong link to the future. Have you ever been so close to something that you could "taste it"? That's the future. The problem with the future, of course, is that it's incredibly fast. This may seem obvious, since it has maintained the ability to stay ahead of the past and the present forever. Yet you constantly see non-ninjas naively assume that they know where the future is headed: Thomas Dewey, Ferdinand von Zeppelin, Dr. Emmett Brown.

To avoid the tragedies of these men and others, a ninja always combines smell and taste into a single sense: smaste. Once mastered, smaste allows the ninja to remember things just before they happen.

How do you acquire this skill without slipping into a temporal vortex of eternal and painful physical deconstruction?

Go camping in a shopping mall the day after Thanksgiving, the busiest shopping day of the year. This is an arena filled with sickeningly potent fabricated nostalgia and extremely powerful predictions of how great your life will be after purchasing high-quality electric shavers and life-changing belts. Your must avoid all the sales, spirit, and sampler trays.

If you can successfully Ninja Camp (see the list below) at a major shopping center on that day without getting caught or killed, you will have reached a solid understanding of your sense of smaste.

For those of you thinking that this endeavor will end up akin to the plots of *Career Opportunities, Mannequin,* or even *Chopping Mall,* you are sorely and quite possibly fatally mistaken. Imagining you are in a 1980s movie is responsible for more than 600 deaths every year.

The Ninja Mall Camping Code: As a ninja, I will do my best to BE UNDETECTED by workers and patrons of the mall, BE CAREFUL with fire, sharp weapons, and sticky foods, BE KILLSERVATION-MINDED.

Remember, this mall did not kill your master or attack your village. You are not here to cause excessive pain and suffering. No-trace camping is supposed to be a fun way to master smaste. Like all fun things, it takes careful, meticulous planning, extreme focus, and constant attention to every single element in your vicinity.

NINJA CAMPING ESSENTIALS (SHOPPING MALL)

- Japanese broadsword forged in a fire of leprechaun bones
- Head-to-toe black clothing
- Map of the mall
- Trifurcated consciousness
- Willingness to kill and dispose of at least four dozen bodies (human or otherwise)
- Wool socks

SMASTE NINJA CAMP CHECKLIST

☐ GET LOST. (Hint: Using a map from a different mall is a great start.) Find your way back to your car using only the memory of where you want to be.

☐ FOOD COURT SLEEPOUT. Must be accomplished within 30 feet of a Sbarro and a bathroom during the lunch hour. No faking it. You must actually enter REM sleep at least four times.

☐ CAMPFIRE. (Silent sing-along optional.) Build a raging bonfire in a very crowded store or theatre without anyone becoming aware of its presence. To accomplish this task, you must smaste the smoke before it is detected by anyone else and cast a disregarder spell to make the patrons ignore the fact that the store (and possibly the patrons as well) are ablaze. Don't feel bad about the body count. This takes a few tries, and remember—just because they don't have the right to shout "Fire" doesn't mean that you can't start one.

☐ NO-TRACE STALKING. Navigate between two major department stores using only your tongue during regular business hours without being noticed. You must stay invisible during this challenge. If you have mastered your sense of smaste, you will be able to use your tongue to tell if someone is looking at you.

☐ TEEN IDENTIFICATION. Lurk near a group of at least six teenage girls and, using only your nose, figure out some way to tell them apart.

☐ S'MORES. S'lesses are unacceptable.

Opinjas: Japan

It's like Hawaii with class.

—Brimstone, age 463

Hands down the least hairy place I have ever lived, and trust me that is a good thing.

—Sea Yew, age 99

Sometimes my boyfriend calls me Chiyo, which is the name of Ziyi Zhang's character from *Memoirs of a Geisha* and she's not even Japanese. It kind of creeps me out, but he's pretty stupid most of the time so, whatever.

—Untamed Heart, age 17

日本について間違っている何でも輸入された。

—Mei Axe Yu, age 124

It just feels like home. A tremendously well-hidden home where no one even knows of your existence.

—Extra Wild, age 45

I do not recognize the borders and establishments of man. That said, great sushi!

—Walloping Swallow, age 23

What do you think?

_____   _____

_____

Nerve Us

Can you fight hand-to-whatever with an 8,000-pound sea urchin shaped like the face of 50 Cent?

Can you tell an adorable baby sea otter that it didn't make the fishball team?

Can you watch two incredibly overweight trolls mate while enduring the sounds of a thousand Ashlee Simpsons?

A ninja can.

When it comes to the sense of nerve, ninjas differ from all other martial artist, ass kickers and most other forms of Killersapiens. Others deaden nerves and build calluses to avoid pain. A ninja heightens his sensitivity and learns to channel the information through all levels of consciousness. Other killers turn things off and feel nothing. Ninjas turn all the switches on and feel everything. This ain't government work. This is ninja life.*

To gain ninja-level nerve, you need to be able to answer yes to but one question: *Can I?* Without hesitation or concern a ninja will always answer yes.

It's important to note that the question is not Will I? or Should I? Or even Can Somebody? It's Can I? If you need more information than those two words, you are not at a ninja level of nerve. Sometimes we know what lies ahead, and it's nasty. Real nasty. Like drinking-alligator-vomit-type nasty. Sometimes we have no idea what challenges or stupidity we will encounter. (An example of this would be illogical.) But disirregardless of any information or experience, the ninja knows he can do it. He can face it. He *can*.

MEASURING NERVE

1. **ATTACH A VERY CLOSE FRIEND** whose deepest, darkest secrets you know to the middle of a tasty dessert (not a desert), surrounded by rabid pigs. (The pigs should be arranged in a circular fashion; see diagram.)

2. **SET UP A CAMERA** and an AV link to all of his/her family, friends, and relevant government agencies.

---

* It is not suggested that you get that tattooed across your abdomen.

3. **REQUIRE FRIEND TO** reveal each and every sick, twisted thought and criminally stomach-turning deed while forcing him/her to punch and kick 90-year-old ladies.

4. **RETURN THE FRIEND** safely home with a chip implanted in his/her head that continually suggests horrifically disgusting random acts for the remainder of his/her life.

5. **CARE VERY DEEPLY** about your friend and feel really, really bad about what you did.

    (Repeat the exercise until you accomplish step 5 in earnest. Note that each time you start again, you will need to choose a new friend.)

If you can successfully complete this exercise, you will be prepared to feel everything.* This

* Ev-ver-ry-thing!

means you can now begin to build up your mental and emotional nerve.

Make a list of things that affect your nerves or that you don't care about. Challenge yourself to overcome at least five of them every day. Copy this work sheet and use it as a helper.

NERVEY ACTIVITIES RECORD

Date: _____ Thing that unnerves me: _____
What I did to make myself feel it at my very essence:

_____

Date: _____ Thing that denerves me: _____
What I did to combat the *heebies* and the *jeebies*:

_____

Date:_____ Thing that werves me: _____
What I did to maintain the cellular integrity of my basic physical form: _____

Date: _____ Thing that querves me: _____
What I did to keep my nerve endings from endlessly questioning everything they feel:

_____

Date: _____ Thing that ughherves me: _____
What I did to not spurl inside my mask:

_____

PHYSICAL NERVE

The physical nerve of a ninja encompasses the basic ability to endure all pain and sense all pleasures and annoyances without ever losing focus. It seems simple, but it should not be taken for granted. A weeklong trek through the Cave of Good Touch Bad Touch will put you in a good position regarding physical nerve . . . or drive you to the brink of complete insanity. Either way, it's a valuable experience that you will never forget.

For psychological reasons, the location of the Cave of Good Touch Bad Touch is undisclosed.

When you think you are ready (you will never actually be ready), sit in a bath of warm bleach and meditate about your mother. A ninja master will collect you in a sack and transport you to the cave. You and/or your remaining parts will be returned to the tub when you are finished.

My most memorable feeling from

the Cave of Good Touch Bad Touch was riding a spiky aardvark that was on fire through a Bette Midler concert while getting a very deep back rub by a gorgeous Swedish supermodel. Even to this day, when I watch the movie *Beaches* my shoulders bleed. But I learned something important in that mystical cavern: What I feel is not nearly as vital as what I *do* with what I feel. I will get approval to kill Ms. Midler one day and nothing conceived by the darkest demon will be able to protect that wretched, red-headed banshee from my methodical wrath.

—Double Water, ninja

WEAPON HIGHLIGHT
SHURIKEN

Contrary to popular myth, not all shurikens are star shaped. Hatori Hanzo simply defines shurikens as "any little pointy thing that I can throw."

The shuriken, like all ninja weapons, was born from necessity. One day a young ninja named Flippy was crossing the countryside to his girlfriend's house, where he had left all of his weapons (he had foolishly taken them off when they were "doing it"). He stumbled upon a recently concluded samurai battle that, like most samurai battles, had left both sides completely dead. Just then, a third samurai army showed up. Through an almost comical exchange of miscommunication, the third group of samurais thought Flippy had killed the other two armies. Enraged, they surrounded Flippy (which made no sense given the fact that they had come there to kill the already dead samurai, but then again, they *were* samurai, so it wasn't that surprising). Flippy looked around for a weapon, but only saw the cheap, mostly broken crap weapons that the dead samurai had been using. He began to pick up whatever he could find and wing it at the 2,000 advancing samurai. In five minutes, they were all dead. The story spread, and within a year every ninja was carrying some sort of bladed throwing weapon.

On the next page, circle all of the things that could be used as shurikens.

You should have circled every thing except Tom Cruise.

SAFE SHURIKEN USE

DO wash all "found" shurikens before use. You don't know where they've been.

DO retrieve your homemade or high-quality shurikens after your adversary is dead. A good shuriken can last you 15 to 20 kills with proper maintenance.

DO be really specific about your target. These things are little. They're a finesse weapon. Throwing at a "werewolf" is not specific enough. "Left werewolf eye as he is facing me" is more like it.

DO warm up before any mission involving shurikens. And keep your shoulder loose. If you throw out your arm on the first toss, the master could take you out for the rest of the mission.

DO join an Ultimate Shuriken team. It's a splendid recreation and a good way to keep up on your technique.

DO NOT carry your shuriken in any sort of case or container. You're gonna need to get to those suckers quickly.

DO NOT make a "cool" *pfft!* sound when you throw your shuriken. Either the shuriken will make it or, best case, it won't. You don't see people with real laser guns shouting *peeuw!* every time they fire.

DO NOT eat fried chicken or other greasy foods while on a mission. Nothing is more embarrassing than the *tink tink* of a dropped shuriken or the look from your fellow ninja whose head your shuriken went into when it slipped out of your hand.

DO NOT limit yourself to throwing shurikens with your hands. You've got a separated big toe in your tabi boots. Can you flex your ears well enough to throw something? Maybe try shooting some classic Nasty Nasal Nails. How about using your mind? Or was it just blown by that idea?

WARNING: Before weapon use, be sure to consult "Weapon Care and Training," page 275.

When I was back rowing crew for my Dievy League College I used to cut tiny holes in my cheeks to hold tiny poisoned spikes. Then, during the race, I would spit them at the opposing coxswain. You can't shout if you can't breathe. I recall often falling asleep to the voice of one crying in the wilderness as the poison wore off.

—Dart Mouth, ninja

The Where of Awareness

Non-ninjas see things, feel things, and sense things. Ninjas and ninjas alone *know* things. How? Because we do. Awareness is not an intellectual state of facts and figures. Awareness is Now. A ninja's sense of awareness comes from knowing what's going on *now*. It is not a mistake that "know" and "now" are separated by but a *k*. Now does not specifically involve or not involve anything. Now is a fluid concept and the core of all awareness. Wherever Now goes, so goes the ninja.

GETTING TO KNOW NOW

After heightening your sense of smaste, you have become comfortable linking the past to the future in the present. But that is neither Now, nor the spirit behind Now. Now is the active state of the present. They may seem similar but they are as different as *Night of the Living Dead* and *Day of the Living Dead*.

Now is only what's happening *now* (note: not

What's Happening Now!!, the spin-off sequel to *What's Happening!!*). Now is the constant definition of life. Now cannot be quantified by time. Before your head explodes from contemplating it, let's get to know Now through some fun challenges.

NOWTIVITIES

1.   Get a buddy and go to the zoo. Ask your buddy to videotape your reactions after you jump into a habitat with at least seven deadly "big cats." (Big cats include lions, tigers, cheaters, cougars, and polar bears.) Watch the tape and notice your reactions as the animals attack. Did you spend too much time dwelling on what had just bit you rather than what was biting you? Did you stay focused on what was attacking you or did your eyes wander to what was about to attack you?

2.   Choose a small public area and claim it as your kingdom. A 10' × 10' square in a park or busy street is usually good. Establish yourself as the supreme ruler and put forth some sort of flag or Coke bottle as your feudal symbol. Declare war on all neighboring land and defend your borders without mercy.

3.   Produce and mount a one-man musical production of the movie *Spider-Man.* You must individually play all of the parts, operate the lights, and play all of the instruments in the orchestra. Do not stop performing the show until you receive at least three positive reviews from local or national reviewers.

4.   Jump out of an airplane at 40,000 feet with a bolt of nylon and a small sewing kit. Fashion yourself a parachute before you hit the ground.

5.   Attend a holiday meal with at least five people over the age of 60. Stay focused and engaged in the conversation from cocktails through dessert with no bathroom breaks. Even when Now is boring, sometimes you have to be there.

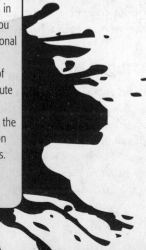

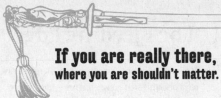

If you are really there,
where you are shouldn't matter.

—Johnathick Snap, ninja

Remember, in order to be ninja-like, you must be aware; and in order to be aware, you must be able to react to anything *as* it is happening. A popular misconception in non-ninja physics is that for every action there is an equal and opposite reaction. Ninjas have discovered that if you are truly aware, there can be an equal and opposite *action* to every action. Taking out the "re" has saved thousands of ninjas from boredom and death. A ninja does not wait for the "re" in order to act. Also, if a ninja is truly in the Now, he can often produce an action that is *greater* than the first action. The more Ninja you become, the more you will realize that most "laws" of science are more like casual suggestions.

The Bleeding Edge

Before attempting the next step on the path, take a few seconds to assess and confirm your worthiness.

MASTER'S WRAP-UP

Schedule a meeting with a ninja master to discuss your progress. Give him a specific time and place for the meeting, but don't show up. If it takes the master longer than one hour to find you and beat you senseless, you are ready to take your next step as a ninja . . . as soon as you can walk again.

CLANVERSATIONS

Discuss the following questions with your clan-mates.

1. Are you looking at me?

2. How can you stalk online without being creepy?

3. Why didn't Leonardo da Vinci write a book called *Jesus Had A Daughter and Here's Where the Proof Is,* instead of painting and hiding things all over Europe?

NINJA PROVERB

shhhhh.
—c. m. cumming

6

Whoooooooo

The Ninja and his apprentice practice an extreme hiding technique called "The Rambo."

Now that you've survived the first three steps on the path, you might be getting a little cocky.

Keep in mind that while you are like a ninja, you're still a long way from becoming a ninja.

Achieving even the rank of Whooooooo is so difficult that a mere word could not contain it—rather, it is pure sound. The sound of a gentle breeze. A very gentle breeze that carries on it an ominous whistle of death like a creepy, unkempt old-timer in a horror movie.

Purse your lips together in a circular shape, leaving just the tiniest hole for air to flow through. Now exhale evenly. Do you hear that sound? That's the next step.

Think of everything you've done so far as learning to play a musical instrument . . . a magical musical instrument whose notes kill things. Your talents are the air whose blowing through that instrument. Your clan by this point is kind of like your band, each person excelling in a different set of skills. Together, hopefully, you "sound" bigger and deadlier than your numbers . . . without actually *making* much sound or being noticed, of course. Now it's time to tighten up that band so that like a former president you can get better gigs and maybe get picked up by a record label. I'm not talking about matching uniforms and groupies. I'm talking about jazz, baby. Taking the flow you know and turning it into art. There is a difference between pulling someone's arm off and flipping him over your head and *pulling someone's arm off and flipping him over your head.* There's a difference between not being there and *not being there.* There is most certainly a difference between a kill and a *kill.*

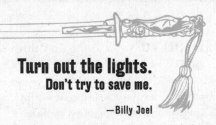

Turn out the lights.
Don't try to save me.

—Billy Joel

Whoooooooo Requirements

As you battle for awesomeness in this chapter, you must also accomplish the requirements below, or so help us, you will not finish the chapter. And by finish, we mean survive.

After accomplishing each challenge, you must make a scroll describing your triumph. Then burn the scroll and eat the ashes (it is okay to mix with happy thoughts if needed).

☐ **1.** Demonstrate your ability to shut the hell up.

☐ **2.** Show how to transport yourself and one other ninja

a. From a rapidly shrinking parallel dimension

b. Through the intestinal tract of a creature in excess of 10,000 pounds

☐ **3.** Successfully complete the nonstop four-month I.O.N. swimmer's test.

☐ **4.** Demonstrate when you should and should not use mercy.

☐ **5.** Identify or show evidence of at least 10 kinds of pure evil found in your community.

☐ **6.** Explain the procedures to follow in the safe handling, storage, and disposal of fresh kills when there is a second kill to be made and you don't want your opponent(s) to get tipped off by the body of the first kill.

☐ **7.** Create a die-orama displaying at least 63 ways to kill something with a cat.

8. Encourage someone who has just started on the Nonja Path by cooking them a meal that uses three deadly poisons.

9. Exhibit determination beyond the bounds of reason.

10. List the five most common signs that something is undeniably dead. Explain the procedures for CPR (Certifying Permanent Repose).

_____

_____

_____

_____

_____

_____

_____

Ninformation

A ninja is only as good as the information he/she/it is working off of. Existence is full of information, and all of it at some point could be useful to a ninja. Therefore, it is vital that a young ninja understands his sources of information and lays out a plan for gathering and using that information.

Once you have gathered information, you should be sure to share that information only when *you* want to share it and with whom you want to share it with. This is the power of secrets (note: not the power of the Secret). Therefore, you should avoid writing any ninformation down whenever possible.

When you absolutely *must* write something down, a good ninja always uses the trusted Invisible Scroll method.

I Wanna Make an Invisible Scroll

First, it should be understood that the scroll is not actually invisible. That is simply a colorful name applied to make it sound more challenging to those who might try and read it.

Let's make one.

1.   **MAKE A SIMPLE** black-skin scroll out of the bark of a melanoid mandrake. (Note: You don't need to kill the mandrake to get this; you merely have to remove its outer epidermal layer.)

2.   **INVENT A LANGUAGE** that you share with no one. It should not contain any known letters, numbers, symbols, or pictures.

3.   **USING RAVEN-FEATHER INK,** write down your important information on the scroll. The ink will only be visible on the mandrake skin under the light of the moon.

4.   **ROLL UP THE** scroll and put it in a safe but easily accessible place. Many ninjas hollow out a portion of a lower rib, while others find small pockets in the space that surrounds them. If you choose the latter, understand that if the air around you is too thick, you will not be able to summon the scroll.

SOURCE	DEFINITION	FILTER
PERSONAL EXPERIENCE	Information you gather from actual circumstances that you physically participate in. (Example: You fight a horde of Amazon vampiresses.)	Your ability to perceive your world.
HEARSAY	Communication from a person about their perceptions of stuff. (Example: "My brother told me about this dude who offed like fifty of these undead lesbos.")	Your ability to interpret the expressions of a third party and wade through their narcissism and insecurities.
MEDITATION	Information you perceive through transcendental means. (Example: While floating outside of your body in a cloud in the Realm of Possibility, you witness a British boys' academy that is secretly run by the Amazon vampiresses as a breeding and feeding factory.)	Your ability to distill the pan-dimensional forces and extraterrestrial participants that influence your perception of an essence.
NINTERNET	Information you receive through the ninja Internet. Although this is also a form of hearsay, the community interactive elements and bullshit make it unique. (Examples: Hot chick sucking and soul-possessing action. —V.I.L.F. Hunter. *Or*: Am I the only one who thinks there is a double standard between people who drink blood and people who eat brains? —ZombieGirl15 *Or*: I am an exiled princess looking to give 10% of my 300 million euros to a disease-free male who weighs at least 200 pounds.)	Your ability to penetrate the lies, deception, temptation, and more lies.

USES	GOOD	BAD
Kicking ass and taking names.	"Been here. Done this. Got the T-shirt and wore it out."	"Holy shit! What the fuck is that?"
Learning from the ass kicking and name taking of others.	"Let's say a little bird told me how to kill you."	"I guess 'pretty cool' to Eddie means sixteen horns that shoot vaporized mercury."
Getting away from the hustle and bustle of your body.	"This beauty is indefinable by my physical senses."	"This all-consuming pain is tearing apart the very fabric of my self."
One-stop shopping for understanding the views and opinions of the entire world.	"ALERT! A fire gnome is summoning the skeleton army of Krakhor to destroy the peaceful village of Hollywood."	"Um, never mind. It was just a mash-up of a NIN video by a 13-year-old with the handle AssANinjerk."

A Time to Kill

Assuming all of your paperwork has been filed with I.O.N.'s Division of Life and approved by a grand master, and you have identified your enemy or target, now what? You're far enough along that literally dozens of unbelievably deathly techniques are racing through your eager brain. What are you going to choose? This is a tough call, but remember: Killing, like comedy, is all in the timing. Choosing *when* you're going to kill something often plays an important role in how you're going to kill it. Here are nine prime moments to take someone out.

1. **RIGHT BEFORE YOUR ENEMY KNOWS YOU'RE THERE.** This may seem obvious, but you'd be quite surprised how many young ninjas think it's fun or cool to deliver a witty remark face-to-face with their foe right before striking: "You killed my brother, prepare to die." "What has two thumbs and a short life span?" "I'm sorry, but I came to break your heart." This is a rookie mistake. Kill. Leave. Reminisce.

2. **RIGHT AFTER YOUR ENEMY HAS EATEN A BIG MEAL.** No one wants to fight with a tummy full of yummy. They want to unbutton their pants and watch reruns of sitcoms and *SportsCenter*. It will really surprise them if they are suddenly watching a kama pull out their intestines.

3. **WHEN YOUR ENEMY IS ON THE POT.** It's old school and dirty, but when they're stopping and plopping, they're ripe for popping and chopping.

4. **RIGHT AFTER SOMEONE ELSE HAS ATTACKED YOUR ENEMY.** The ninja is not afraid of a hard day's work, but if someone wants to do half the work for you, great. It's usually easier to fight an enemy who has one arm than one who has two. The same goes for legs, eyes, ears, kidneys, lungs, and hips. Just make sure you actually do the killing. Take pride in your work, and don't leave the actual death dealing to someone else. Remember, you're striving to be a ninja, not a Bond villain.

5. **RIGHT AFTER YOUR ENEMY HAS BEEN DUMPED.** Emotional distress in general can be an asset, but it is also as unreliable as Michael Mann

movies. You never really know what you're going to get. The most reliable form of distress for killing is that which occurs after the harsh breakup. Heck, often the victim wants to die. But, either way, he will be way too busy replaying every moment of the last six months to put up much of a fight. The most prime moment to strike in these situations is right as your enemy picks up the phone to call the ex and beg for one more chance.

6. **WHEN YOUR ENEMY IS SLEEPING.** You know, because they're not awake.

7. **RIGHT AFTER YOUR ENEMY HAS KILLED SOMEONE.** You have to be quick here because their adrenaline will be pumping, but most non-ninjas will take a deep breath of satisfaction right after they defeat a difficult foe. This is a great moment to shove something sharp in their head. Pay attention after you kill them, as someone might be planning to employ this same technique on you.

8. **RIGHT BEFORE YOUR ENEMY FINISHES A JOKE.** It is truly remarkable what people will ignore to get out a punch line. When attempting this kill, it's essential that you do *not* prevent the victim from delivering the punch line with their final breath. This way, those listening to the joke will be too busy laughing to notice that the joke teller is having a very jagged dagger shoved up his nose. Plus you are there to kill the comedian not the comedy. *WARNING:* Listen carefully to the setup. If the joke seems like it's going to be a dud, abort. This kill does not work without irony.

9. **WHEN YOUR ENEMY IS EXTREMELY OLD.** Old people are often weaker and frailer than younger people. Be sure to check your enemy's medical records before deciding on this kill and keep in mind that not all things age at the same rate.

Remember that an enemy can only kill you if it is not dead. (Note: Zombies and vampires are not dead. They are either the undead or the living dead. Big difference.) Therefore, your goal is to make that enemy dead as quickly as possible. Don't get too caught up in the above techniques as hard and fast rules. Your job is not the process, it's the outcome: swift and fearsome death for all who oppose you. Also, be considerate of your fellow ninja: Do not rely on any of these moments too often. If lots of people start getting offed right after they get dumped, the general world of enemies will begin to avoid long-term relationships, and you will ruin that technique for everyone.

The lepretaur is known for bribing enemies with "fool's gold" made from his own feces. A ninja who knows this will use moment number three to strike this hoofed huckster.

Threats

Occasionally, a master will order you to give something a warning rather than just kill it. Maybe the creature is rare or adolescent. In these instances, rare or adolescent as they may be, you must be prepared to deliver a high-quality threat that will garner the desired result. Keep in mind this is a threat that you want to use for behavioral modification, not for inciting an altercation. If you fight, someone is going to die and that is not what we want . . . in this situation.

Whenever possible, a threat should be:

• Personal

• Forceful

• Witty

• Biologically specific

Practice your threats by coming up with your own versions of the samples that follow. Remember that the threat should change depending on the creature you're threatening. If you tell a garuda* that you're going to strangle him with his own tentacles, he'll laugh and say, "Well then, I guess I'm safe until I happen to grow tentacles." Nothing undercuts a threat like ignorance. Also, the victim has to really think you mean it. Think back to when your gym teacher would yell and yell and yell about wearing a protective cup, but never really do anything. A ninja does nothing idly, and that goes double for threats.

Note, this is not Mad Libs. This is a dangerous

---

* A large birdlike creature with a violent sense of humor.

and exacting task that requires your utmost focus and intelligence.

1. If you don't stop I am going to shove your _____ so far up your _____ you're gonna be able to use your _____ as a _____.

2. Oh, it's not me I'm worried about. It's my sword here. See, it's got a nasty habit of _____.

3. I'd tell you to ask someone, but unfortunately all of them are _____.

4. I have a DVD player, lots of free time, and the complete film works of _____ (e.g., Sandra Bullock).

5. The last time I pulled out my _____ the police had to go all the way to _____ to retrieve the other half of the _____.

6. You have a nice set of _____. I wonder what they'd look like hanging from my rearview mirror.

7. I don't know if you remember how the movie _____ ends, but unless you _____ I will make sure you don't.

8. The way I see it, you've got two options. You can keep on _____ or you can live until tomorrow.

9. You will stop _____ right now—unless, of course, you want to eat the rest of your meals through your _____.

10. You know what the difference is between you and a _____? A _____ doesn't have to ring a bell every time it has to pee.

Opinjas: Femininjas

If you're really a ninja, I shouldn't be able to tell your gender.

—Count It, age 19

All I know is that I can hide one more sword than the boy ninjas.

—The Cut, age 25

Honestly, my wife is way more bendy than me. High five.

—Scorpion Pillow, age 35

Where do I start? They're distracting. They way overthink shit. And did you know that their "monthly visitor" attracts dragons? I tell ya, the last thing I need is some chick checking her eyeliner in her katana instead of thrusting it through that wyvern behind me.

—Bane Bo, age 198

There's still discrimination. I can't remember the last time I was sent to kill something with more than one head.

—Nelly Nunchuck, age 29

All I'm asking for are smaller guis for 'em, or, you know . . . Do they really even need the top half?

—Jake the Snake, age 41

What do you think?

_____

_____

Ninja Profiles

In order to help you fully appreciate how far you have yet to go, several ninja profiles are included below. They will remind you how not-ninja you truly are, yet also give you fantastic insights that your head oatmeal would never be able to conjure on its own.

There is no such thing as an average ninja. Every ninja must be supreme. If you have trouble with the idea that multiple entities could each individually be supreme, you understand neither ninjaness nor supremacy and will most likely perish soon from your ignorance. According to a recent ninja study, knowing is 43.7 percent of the average battle. Since battles are like ninjas in the fact that there is no such thing as an average one, it is highly suggested that you review the following profiles with the hope of knowing even a minuscule amount more about ninjas that you currently do.

NAME: MOSES DEAF

SPECIAL SKILLS: SUPER SMASTE

ANECDOTE: In 1803, a blind and deaf ninja with a detached nervous system set out on a three-year practical joke to confuse and annoy pioneer explorers Lewis and Clark. Using only his sense of smaste, Moses Deaf thoroughly messed with the gentlemen throughout their interior journey and on both the Missouri and Columbia rivers. His documentation, written with his nose in 1809 in the blood of Meriwether Lewis, won two Killutzer Prizes and is considered one of the funniest ninja books ever.

PERSONAL COMMENTS (communicated entirely with his sense of smell): "If you could see what I smaste, you would all go quite mad. Quite mad indeed."

NAME: BLACK EYES

SPECIAL SKILLS: SUPER WATCHER, SURVEILLANCE

ANECDOTE: He once saw Phil Collins singing "In the Air Tonight" *while* drowning a man.

PERSONAL COMMENTS: "Even if you think, 'This guy has never even seen me,' I probably have. That's what I do. I watch, I look, and, to the extent that man can, I like to think that I see. Do I have my favorite people to watch? Sure. I suppose that's unavoidable. I imagine scientists have favorite stars to gaze at, frogs to dissect, or letters to theorize about. As you might guess, I like to watch strippers, but I bet it's not for the reason you think. Boobs are amazing for sure, but it's what's behind those boobs that really intrigues me. Do you know that on average a professional stripper in Las Vegas tells 415 lies every single shift? On nights when they're not working, even more. Strippers are masters of lies. If you're a sailor, they sail every weekend with their girlfriends. If you like Russian women, so do they. If you can't forget 'Nam, neither can they . . . kissing their girlfriends kind of helps, though. When you start a non-ninja team of covert secret operatives, it's hard to beat strippers. Forget James Bond. He's terrible. Everyone figures out his cover in like two seconds, his gadgets are like Flintstone technology and the tuxedo is quite possibly the least appropriate mission outfit ever. I have watched actual, real-life British double-O spies, and he's a pretty accurate picture. If strippers could organize themselves outside of Teasey's Nightclub, I am quite convinced they would have their own country. Who else do I like to watch? Zoo people are good. The things they say to animals. Wow. Animals, as you may have experienced, have no problem acting real. Perhaps that is why most people tell their deepest and darkest fears and truths to cats and dogs."

NAME: THE HUSHER

SPECIAL SKILLS: SILENTEST OF THE SILENT ASSASSINS

ANECDOTE: His ringtone is Rod Steiger's silent scream from the 1964 drama *The Pawnbroker.*

PERSONAL COMMENTS (written by Terror Tear): "I am writing the following message on behalf of The Husher, who is so committed to silence he won't even write something down. As one of his best friends, I can honestly say that I have never heard him. He communicates entirely in noiseless pain, which, unlike a flourless cake, is just as good, if not better, than the conventional version. It really is the most powerful way to convey any message. If you don't think silence is a mighty tool, just ask The Husher about it. He won't answer you . . . and then you'll die. He's a master of silence. If you need something made quiet, all you have to do is just not say the word and he'll quiet it. And, he'll do it using every tool in the deadly ninja basket of death. He can break a leg in two without the leg or the leg owner uttering a single peep. I have personally seen him throw a banshee off a 20-story building. She didn't make a sound on the way down or when she hit. That's impressive, because one of the main things banshees do is wail all the time. Some people say that The Husher is too quiet. But, of course, talking like that just makes it easier for him to find them and shut them up.

"The Husher actually absorbs sound. The technique is called Black Sound. His most recent mission involved infiltrating a coven of villainous librarians who lived in a cave lined with Bubble Wrap. He was able to dispatch all of them by—he would like me to stop writing this now. Shhhh."

NAME: THE FURY

SPECIAL SKILLS: HE DOESN'T REALLY WANT TO TALK ABOUT 'EM

ANECDOTE: Has received more Ninja Of The Year awards than any other living ninja and is number four on the all-time record list for Killing Things Behind You Without Looking.

PERSONAL COMMENTS: [*Loud sigh. "The Shade of Poison Trees," by Dashboard Confessional, plays in background*] "Oh, you don't want to know about me. I'm just a ninja. Nothing special. I do my thing. I make my kills. Oh, I shouldn't even be writing this, but they asked me to, so I do it. What is there to say about me? I have never done anything that a thousand other ninjas haven't done a thousand times. *(Exhale)* So, what am I supposed to tell you about? Erghh. I don't know. I mean, it's a darn dark world. Yeah. You know what I mean? It's really dark. Not like all the darkness that we know about. I mean the other darkness. The black abyss inside. You know?

"People obsess about dark matter and what its purpose is for in the universe. At least dark matter has a name. At least it has wonder and light to define it. But not this other darkness thing that I'm talking about. In here. And I'm not even pointing to anything when I say that. My whole inside is dark. Beyond my blood and guts and bone and brain, there is a darkness. An indefinable void of blacker than black. I hate this darkness and it hates me. Like the seething stare-down between two double-eyed fire ferrets* with a sliced banana between them. Nothingness like nothing minus nothing times nothing divided by the inverse absence of nothing plus a punch in the gut. It consumes me, but it never stops devouring, as if it is secretly creating more of me each day for it to eat. Perhaps it did make me. Maybe that is why I know it without ever seeing it. It is my ninja. Or is every ninja the product of this mass of absence, and is all

---

* One of eight types of flaming rodents including: frats, frabbits, prairie fire dogs, glowing gophers, charchillas, flamsters, and porcupyres.

we do in pursuit of our maker? At least then I would have someone to share this soul-sucking emptiness with. Perhaps, more likely, I am alone the keeper of this darkness. A punished existence as the vessel of the unknown and unimaginable ennui. Ennui, that's sadness, fear, apathy, anger, helplessness, and confusion, right?

"I'm sorry. My words are failing me. This is the first time I have ever really expressed these . . . what? I don't know . . . thoughts? I should not have done this. The darkness feels stronger now. Oh, what have I done? I don't know. Maybe I have to bring the pulsing, torturous black to the surface to expel it. Or, maybe this is all a ploy by the darkness to take me over once and for all? Why do I have to know of black and shadow and uneverything? *(Exhale) (Sigh)* You know what? I'm glad I wrote this. Now, no matter what happens, there will be this . . . whatever."

NAME: CRAVEN LAVA

SPECIAL SKILLS: SICK HOT, CAN PUNCH THROUGH ALMOST ANYTHING FROM ONE INCH AWAY

ANECDOTE: Once while she was completely hidden from view, her mere presence made a homosexual wizard ejaculate twice.

PERSONAL COMMENTS: "I guess I'm pretty. I've never really thought about it. All I know is that I spent many years training in the deadly art of sexy. It's not conceited for me to say that I know how to work *It* because I know I do. *It* is my special thing. Wanna see my *It?* I can tell you with sexertainty, no, you don't. I have worked *It* right through a grown man's chest. You could've fit a good-sized cantaloupe through the hole. I made a fachen* snap its own neck by walking around him doing this thing with my hips that I can do. Do you understand? I not only sexually enticed a creature with absolutely no biological similarities or chance for procreation with me, but I made it so 'into' me that it chose death over looking away. It would have taken that silly creature a mere moment to whip his head around in the opposite direction and catch me coming around from the other side. I'm sorry, honey, but that is dead sexy.

"Also, I want you to think about something, 98 percent of my body is covered. Less is more. These days, in a few clicks, you can see anybody doing anything completely naked. But you can't see my body business. And that is just one reason why it is the thing most desired. I may be a hottie, but I'm a ninja, baby. You're not seeing me unless I want you to, and I probably don't want you to unless I also want you dead. And when I do show you something, it won't be much. I can kill with a look, a smile, a shimmy, a pout, a turn, a bend . . . the list is quite endless. Gyrating? Cutie, I make

* Although this giant, cyclopean birdish beast has only one leg and a mangled arm jutting from its torso, it is quite sneaky and vicious and has a ravenous appetite for apples and tourists.

Shakira* look like a badly burned Kevin James smothered in Camembert cheese. I'm not being boastful. I'm just telling you, I know how to move my junk and how to move others over to a little place called dead. And, I look good doing it. Double kisses."

NAME: CHI CHI GASHANTE

SPECIAL SKILLS: MASTER OF WEAPONS

ANECDOTE: Once killed 800 Vikings in one day using 800 different weapons, a long-standing ninja record.

PERSONAL COMMENTS: "Weapons to me are like the toppings next to the soft-serve machine at Hometown Buffet—and I'm the ice cream (chocolate). I already taste great, but they make me taste even better. And, just like toppings, you can never add too many weapons.

"On every mission, I carry between 1,400 and 3,000 different weapons. Some are similar with different purposes, like Sclissors (really sharp scissors for cutting off ears and skin folds) and Shlears (really sharp shears for jamming in nostrils and cutting up cartilage). Some weapons are very different but have similar uses. For example, when battling a Big Blue Ox,[†] I might use a Spatulaxe or a Bladed Lasso to remove its ice tail. Some weapons are just weird, like a Harpunn, which is a very ironic spear attached to a cord of wit. When landed successfully in the funny bone of most creatures, it will make them die from amusement as you 'reel' them in.

"Although I enjoy killing with any instrument of death, my personal favorites are: (1) Unlucky Rabbit's Foot: It's enchanted and powerful, but you have to get in very close to use it, and it takes incredible finesse to wield it correctly without any of the bad luck getting on you. (2) Thingamabob: No amount of training can prepare you for this ever-changing weapon. Only the handle stays constant. You have to be ready for fire, sharp edges, poisonous hoses, bloated ex-child stars, or any other dangerous thing to pop out of its hilt. (3) Double Cross Bow: One of the very few weapons that actually works best when handed over to your enemy. The only way to describe the joy of watching something unwittingly kill itself is that feeling you get when someone scores on himself in air hockey.

"I could literally talk for weeks about the wonder of weapons, but like the blues, you will never understand it until you live it. To start finding the weapons that make you happy, I suggest getting one of my three published scrolls: *Killer Things That Kill, Wielding for Dummies,* or *The Encyclopedia of Death.*"

---

* An oil-covered Columbian-Lebanese succubus.
[†] A very very large ox . . . that's blue.

WEAPON HIGHLIGHT

SMOKE BOMB

Many of you may be furrowing your brow asking, "Is that really a weapon?" You bet your black ass it is. Anything that gives you an advantage over your enemy is a weapon.

A good smoke bomb emits a generous plume of thick smoke that completely masks your next movement. Master Fig Leaf once described smoke as "a three-dimensional shadow."

SAFE SMOKE BOMB USE

DO keep them in a safe and *separate* part of your gui. If they get poked and go off inside your clothes, it's gonna be embarrassing for everyone.

DO make sure to remember which hidden pouch has the Illusion Smoke Bombs and which hidden pouch has the Sarin Gas Smoke Bombs.

DO always throw *between* you and your adversary. Otherwise, you're just showing them some smoke.

DO use outside of missions in awkward social situations. It's good practice. Ask any woman, "When's your baby due?" Smoke bomb!

DO NOT be where you were when you threw the smoke bomb once the smoke clears.

DO NOT use against things that can't see.

DO NOT use colored smoke! This is a ninja mission, not an off-the-strip Vegas magic act.

DO NOT mix up with regular bombs.

DO NOT use when meditating on parallel planes of consciousness. You're already not there. Where are you not going to go to?

Bad smoke bomb.

Good smoke bomb.

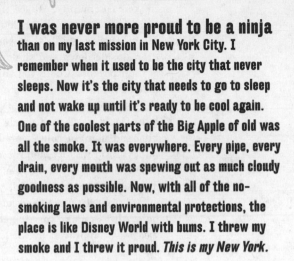

I was never more proud to be a ninja than on my last mission in New York City. I remember when it used to be the city that never sleeps. Now it's the city that needs to go to sleep and not wake up until it's ready to be cool again. One of the coolest parts of the Big Apple of old was all the smoke. It was everywhere. Every pipe, every drain, every mouth was spewing out as much cloudy goodness as possible. Now, with all of the no-smoking laws and environmental protections, the place is like Disney World with bums. I threw my smoke and I threw it proud. *This is my New York.*

—Mountain Scar Slay Seas, ninja, filmmaker

WARNING: Before weapon use, be sure to consult "Weapon Care and Training," page 275.

Communinja Service

Masters have noticed that many ninjalike pursuers begin to withdraw from others at during the Whoooooooo portion of the path. This needs to be avoided. Isolation is a great training tool, but too much time alone can make you weird. More important, the International Order of Ninjas is a community, a community that likes to help other communities whenever communally possible. You are now part of the I.O.N. community, but also still kind of a member of the community you were in before joining the ninja community. That's a lot of communing.

Look for ways that you can reach out as a ninja to your community. Maybe not a lot of people in your area are recycling. Could you make them? Maybe there's a bully that won't stop turning children upside down and shaking the valuables out of their pockets. Could you shake something valuable out of him? Maybe there's a mom that thinks she's a good cook but makes everything taste like hair. Could you sneak meals to her children and husband using a complicated system of signals, pulleys, and well-trained raccoons?

These are just a couple ideas. If you look around your neighborhood, you will notice dozens of circumstances that could use a little ninja help. Always make sure to get all community service ideas approved by an I.O.N. master before starting.

Here's an inspiring letter from a ninjalike boy in San Francisco, California.

Dear Master Yuthinaysha,

I have an idea for a swell community service project. Most people in my community have no idea how deadly ninjas are. I suppose that's fine and makes our job easier. But last night I found my little sister crying in to her pillow. She was scared that the prisoners in San Quentin (a jail near my house) were going to break out and sodomize her.

I'm sure you are aware that there are a small but vocal group of non-ninja sickos that think that they are the best killers in the world. They are obnoxious and rude and give killing a bad name. I am talking, of course, about mass murderers. These dumbheads actually believe that their mode of killing is brilliant. Really? I wonder how many of them have ever killed something more difficult than a human, who, as far as I can tell so far in my training, is one of the easiest animals to kill. According to my *Manual of Demising,* humans make up less than 5 percent of all ninja assassinations. I would love to see David Berkowitz face down even a fir bolg like I did on

my last clan overnight. That Irish giant would be dining on his
Brooklyn butt before he got a shot off.

As an aspiring ninja, I am frustrated by the amateur and
mentally unstable assassins plaguing my community and want to
do something to help.

Here's the plan for my community service project. I plan
to write intelligently worded letters to every mass murderer
at San Quentin. I will explain to them why they are pathetic
cheeseheads and why they will never be counted among the
great masters of death. Using my threat training, I then plan
to describe in colorful detail how I will kill them if they
attempt to continue their silliness. To complete the project, I
will sneak into San Quentin and remove a finger from each person I sent a letter to. I will then mail it back to them with
the word "More?" burned on to it.

I am really stoked about this project and really think it
could help my community and make my sister smile.

Please see my attached Community Service Planning Form and
a list of murderers I plan to contact. I await your response in
deadly silence.

Smoke bomb!
Andy Greenfield

Recently, Andy successfully completed his
project and earned his community service merit
badge. According to his follow-up report, two of the
inmates actually shit themselves when he snuck
into their cells and cut off their fingers. Way to
go, Andy!

What will your project be?

The Bleeding Edge

Before attempting the next step on the path, take a few seconds to assess and confirm your worthiness.

MASTER'S WRAP-UP

Meet with a ninja master and discuss your progress in a theoretical realm that consists only of dark matter. Wrestle with the very truth of your being.

CLANVERSATIONS

Discuss the following questions with your clanmates.

1. If you were a deadly weapon, what weapon would you be and why?

2. Was it me?

3. Is this the best use of my time right now?

NINJA PROVERB

Death will never be dead to me.
It's my life.

—Killie Go Strongarm, ninja

7

I.T.A.N.
(Is That a Ninja)

The Ninja's apprentice fearlessly battles through the backdraft of a Fire Ape.

The I.T.A.N. rank is the highest level a non-ninja can achieve. Those who attain this honor will often be mistaken for ninjas by actual ninjas. Many do not realize that about the name of the rank—it's not a feeble homo lameian wondering "is that a ninja," but rather an actual flippin' *ninja* who's not sure whether or not you're a ninja.

Think about that for a moment. A few years ago, when you started this book, you could barely tell a gwyllion* from a nagumwasuck,† never mind how to kill either of them. Now you're entertaining the idea of fooling real live ninjas!

By now, death and sneakiness are regular parts of your day. You are always on the lookout for ways to make your life, your missions, and your self more ninja-y. Not dying by these high standards is a personal choice and something only a grand master can truly measure. But at this point, many "regular" people should be not-seeing qualities in you that don't let them know you are choosing the ninja way.

You will notice that on this leg of the path there is much less mollycoddling and explaining. A ninja needs to be able to figure out tasks and challenges on their own.

A recent I.T.A.N. attempter described his first day seeking the rank of I.T.A.N. as "Aghhhhhhhhh! Please, God, make it stop!" Since that was also his last day of anything, it seems a good reminder to keep your entire ability to perceive on a swivel. You're playing with the big boys now.

It's go time. Do or die. Kill or be killed.

I need to run every day.
If I don't I feel cheated.

—Joan van Ark

---

* An extremely ugly female spirit and one of very few ghosts that can get drunk.
† An extremely ugly male spirit known for looking at things "weird" or "funny."

I.T.A.N. Requirements

As you battle for awesomeness in this chapter, you WILL accomplish the requirements below, or so help us, you will not finish the chapter.

After accomplishing each challenge, you must make a scroll describing your triumph. Then burn the scroll and eat the ashes (it is okay to mix with a Muse song if needed).

☐ **1.** Be.

☐ **2.** Do.

☐ **3.** Know.

☐ **4.** Kill.

☐ **5.** Hide.

☐ **6.** Move.

☐ **7.** Deal.

☐ **8.** Live.

☐ **9.** Personal measurements:

Heart Rate: Slow _____ beats/year.
Fast _____ hundred beats/second.
Silence: _____ negative decibels.
Will: _____ pounds of resolve.
Honor: _____ ninjas that know and respect me.
Pain: I wouldn't reveal a ninja secret unless they stuck a flaming _____ in my _____.

The Quest of the Best

From your first den stalk to a jungle battle with crapes,* missions are ninjaing at its best. A mission includes everything from planning the mission with an XB-360 Green Planning Workbook and Application Forms to writing a detailed account of everything that happened on the mission on a MRE-78 Fire Form in triplicate.

But most important, no mission is a success if the Mission Code of the ninja has been violated.

THE MISSION CODE

As a ninja, I will:

BE SILENT.

BE SNEAKY as a memory.

BE DEADLY as death.

BE KILLSERVATION-MINDED.

A ninja never kills for recreation
or amusement, only for honor and practice.

—Plugger, ninja

MISSION ETHICS

1. **PLAN AHEAD AND PREPARE.** If you dare to step outside the bounds of honor held sacred by the International Order of Ninjas and try

---

* A breed of giant ape with wings and crane heads.

some stupid, glory-grabbing cowboy crap,
I.O.N. will find you so fast and kill you so slow
that you will actually wish you were watching
an Adam Sandler movie marathon.

2.   **TRAVEL UNDETECTED.** From the moment
you leave your cave or apartment, a ninja
should move with the utmost stealth. If traveling by car, cling to the bottom; if traveling
by plane, hide in the landing gear; if traveling
by wind, hide in a cloud. No one should know
where you are until you're there—and, if possible, not even then.

3.   **KILL IN, KILL OUT.** A long-standing tradition
with ninjas. Do not leave your shurikens in
heads or darts in hearts or kyoketsu-shogeis
in calves. It is not the maid's job to clean up
your discarded weapons. Especially if you've
killed the maid. A ninja is bound to encounter
a guard or a curious house cat on many a mission. If you dispatch these creatures, make
sure you take the tools used for dispatching
them with you or return them to the kitchen
or toolshed or rumpus room before leaving
the area.

4.   **HIDE WHAT YOU KILL.** They may be dead,
but they still physically exist. A good ninja
always stows his kills "out of the way," at
least until the mission is over. Occasionally,
at the discretion of the mission master, you
will be asked to return with a head or a liver
or a whole body for the purposes of breaking
a spell or saving a dimension made of dreams.
Make sure to memorize or bring a small list
of what you are supposed to bring back and
hide or demolish everything else. Completely
obliterated men tell no tales.

5. **MINIMIZE IMPACT.** Why punch something really hard when you can just snap its neck? A punch may make your victim fly backward and crash into something. Why use your katana when the nostril hair of death technique will do? Disemboweled intestines are really hard to get off carpet. That is just the type of noise and unnecessary destruction a ninja tries to avoid. This is not a Jerry Bruckheimer film.

6. **YOU ARE AN UNINVITED GUEST.** This is not your house or office building or underwater cave. Do not "hang out" or "look around" once the mission is over. A ninja is a citizen of the world, but that does not mean that you have the right to play with a gong gong's* nine-headed pet snake right after shooting your long-bow through his chest. A ninja finds himself in a lot of cool places, but, like Alanis Morissette, places only stay cool if you don't touch them.

7. **BE CONSIDERATE OF OTHER NINJAS.** If a mission takes you to London, your job is not to kill the entire city. You probably have one or two things to kill. Remember that other ninjas might be in London at the same time killing other things. The techniques you use could affect their death dealing. If you come across another ninja while on a mission, engage him in a quick but intricate fight to prove you are both real ninjas, draw the weapon you plan to use for your kill, stare him deeply in the eye with fury, smile at him with your eyes, and

---

* A nine-headed water god with the body of a snake. They like to keep snakes as pets and emphatically point out to guests how different they are from them. Also called the "crybabies" of the gods.

then pretend like you hear someone coming and disappear.

Without a Trace

Killing so that you leave no trace shows that you care about the environment—and that you know how to travel through it secretly. When your missions take you to hostile or dangerous places, you need to draw as little attention as possible to yourself and your purpose. *For there was once a ninja named Mount Me who was challenged by her master to steal back the Bitchin' Goat of Kato from a rock band made up of 14 furious guard dawgs* while they were on tour in Haiti. In the middle of their first sold-out free concert, Mount Me jumped up onstage disguised as a One Dollar Bill and instantly started a full scale riot. She then quickly slipped backstage, changed her disguise to Nicole Kidman, and shoved the Bitchin' Goat of Kato up her nose. The Goat, as one might expect, immediately started loudly bitching about the cramped conditions, yucky sticky stuff, and poor room service. Mount Me calmly walked past the band and into the Dominican Republic without incident. Everyone she passed was quite convinced that the sounds they heard were the regular racist, elitist rantings of Nicole Kidman toward the Haitians.*

PERSONAL CLEAN-UP KIT

SLIME: A living gelatinous organism made up of 96 percent lime. It can devour and disintegrate 1 million times its own body weight in 15 minutes. If you have the time, a one-pound Slime is hard to beat.

FORMULA 4,563: Just spray it. It knows what to do.

ELVEN LOCAL 318: They are unionized, but they fit easily in any gui and can rebuild anything overnight.

OXICLEAN: Hey, the stuff works.

* All the ineptness of a security guard combined with someone who likes to be called "dawg."

Eye-Dentification

It's pretty easy to tell a ninja from a non-ninja based on skills and backflips, but telling ninjas apart from one another can be tricky. Since most ninjas cover 99 percent of their body in black 99 percent of the time, they have a tendency to "all look the same." Of course, they are *not* all the same, and if you want to make any ninja friends—even if you want to make any specific ninja enemies (not recommended)— you need to be able to tell them apart. In the ninja world, mistaking one ninja for another is akin to asking a nonpregnant lady when she's due or accusing a handicapped person of faking it.

This exercise will help you develop the skills to tell your ninja brethren (and sistren and thingren) apart. Simply match the name of each famous ninja with his/her/its deadly eyes.

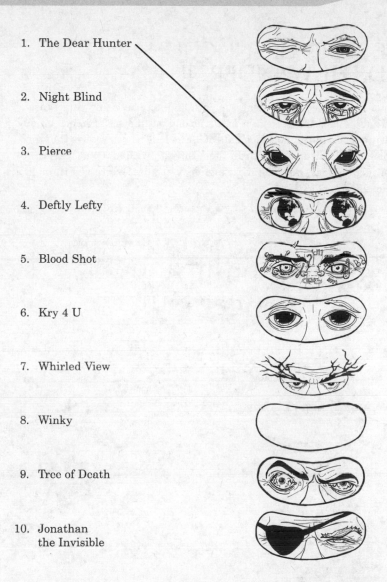

1. The Dear Hunter

2. Night Blind

3. Pierce

4. Deftly Lefty

5. Blood Shot

6. Kry 4 U

7. Whirled View

8. Winky

9. Tree of Death

10. Jonathan the Invisible

THE STORY OF SNUGGLE SNUFF AND THE WONDER NUT

You have experienced much along the path and may be losing your sense of trust. That's a good thing. A ninja trusts no one but himself. Friends, family, and partners are all valuable elements of life as long as you realize that there may come a day when you have run them through with an Orc Cleaver.

Trust is a big idea, but, like most big ideas, it's best expressed through a simple children's story.

Snuggle Snuff and the Wonder Nut

Once upon a time there was a little ninja rabbit named Snuggle Snuff.

One day while coming home from eviscerating a goofy fox, Snuggle Snuff saw a bright light coming from a dark cave.

When Snuggle Snuff hopped in to investigate, he found the Magical Wonder Nut of Yucapi.

When he showed his new prize to the old and wise Professor Carrote, he was told that whoever possesses the Wonder Nut will have unimaginable wealth and eternal kickassitude.

Soon all of the other bunnies became jealous of Snuggle Snuff. They coveted his Wonder Nut and looked at him funny. This made Snuggle Snuff unable to trust anyone.

S o he brutally slew everyone in Hoppy Town and lived happily ever after.

WORKBOOK

1. What can't you trust with anyone else?
2. What method would you use to kill those you do not trust?
3. What would you be willing to do to possess a Wonder Nut of your own?

Hell Hop

Hey, gather up your clan and play a fun game of Hell Hop. The game board has been provided below. The rules are . . . there are no rules. Just survive.

Flaming pine-cones in your anus	Delimbed by four pain cobras	Seven minutes in heaven with a gorgon	Your gui is soaked in mercury	Vampire centaur's bite	Swallowed by a spike-throated slug
You're stuck in a troll mosh pit	Mouthful of black widows	Boiled in magma	But first the aristocrats	Bizzaro You snapped your neck	Infected mermaid orgy
Eaten by zombies	Impaled on a pike	You have died of dysentery	Skinned alive and rolled in salt	Sewn to a dragon's taint	Unicorn horn through your head
You swallowed a dehydrated werewolf	A boa constrictor and a rat catch you napping	A puck plucked your eyes out	Stung by killer killer bees	You die Catherine the Great style but with a squid	Picked apart by vultures
Fed through a woodchopper feetfirst	Buried alive 300 feet deep in Antarctica	Chupacabras are sucking you	Crocagator death roll	Laser slicer	Bone-splitting spikes
Raped by a manticore	Kraken got your tongue	Thrown in a sack with a wolverine	Date with an Italian woman	Ball peen hammered everywhere	Beaten to death with own limbs by ogre

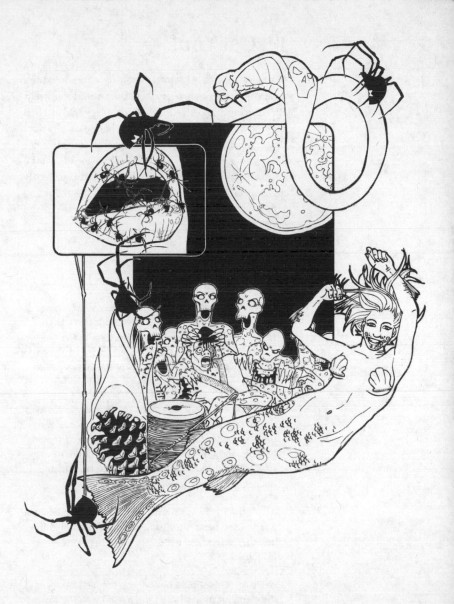

I'll Get You!

Many people think that avenging their master's death is a solo sport. In fact, it can make a great clan outing and a good way for everyone to earn the You Killed My Master merit badge as a group. Since you know that emotions will be running hot once you arrive at the murderer's locale, make sure you take time as a team to plan out the deadly mission of honor. Before you throw one throwing knife, everyone should know his or her role in the operation.

KEY ROLES FOR REVENGING AND AVENGING

RECONJA: This participant needs to come busting through the doors of your clan hideout badly beaten. He should have irrefutable confirmation of the true killer's identity (it will surprise you) and, if at all possible, schematics and blueprints of the killer's whereabouts.

FORENJA: This person stands up with fury in his eyes and makes an impassioned speech that rouses everyone's vehemence and dedication. The speech should also outline a few of the broad strokes of the revenge (e.g., "We will cut off his head and use his skull to make grand toasts to Master Blah Blah Blah!").

AMBIENJAS: This is a small team that should be "the good of the best." They will battle/keep occupied the guards/students/minions, etc., while the Avenja does his job.

AVENJA: This should not only be the best fighter in the clan, but must also be the person with the closest (yet most turbulent) relationship with the slain master. No matter how easy a kill it may be, the Avenja must continue fighting the enemy until he can satisfactorily kill his foe with poetic justice and melodrama.

LAMJA:* If you really want an avenging to remember, you can also incorporate a Lamja. One clan member can offer to be fatally/near-fatally wounded while saving the life of the Avenja during the Avenja's altercation with the murderer. This usually only works if the Lamja has already defeated the murderer's second in command.

The unexamined death
is not worth killing for.

—Sock You Right in the Teeth, ninja philosopher

* Optional, but very cool.

The Hate of Your Life

Spend two days staring through everyone and everything you see with a molten, unhallowed glare of hatred. Do not retreat your despising glance or break eye contact for any reason (grandmother, brick wall, cat, potted plant, sandwich, etc.). Now, ninjas do not hate many things at all, but to *look* as if you do is very important. You are going to be facing creatures that defy reason and sanity. You need to be able to gaze with fury at the most absurd, villainous, and plain-wrong beast. How about a baby deer that has been put through an evilizer machine (see image below). It's not her fault, but you may have to kill her. Can you stare this down?

An evilized baby deer sniffs for innocence.

What Don't You Buy the Ninja Who Can Kill Everything

Once you are a I.T.A.N., you'll find that there are very few things you can't do. The world is your pizza. You'll have so many options that it's easy to get confused. Therefore, the prepared student will start thinking about things you *don't* want.

Make a comprehensive list of everything you don't want to do in your life. Be specific. Don't just put "I don't want to get married." Name names. "I don't want to marry Shasta Cross" or "I don't want to get married unless it is to Hilary or Haylie Duff."

The Ask A Ninja ninja has offered a peek at a very small portion of his list as an example and an encouragement. According to him, he still adds to his list of don'ts every day.

4,568.   I don't want to feel guilty about taking the last of anything at a party. Especially when I've only had like two of 'em all night.

4,569.   I don't want fries with that.

4,570.   I don't want to find out that Michael Cera is not a nice person.

4,571.   I don't want to turn into my dad.

4,572.   I don't want it all to be a dream.

4,573.   I don't want every snowflake to be different.

4,574.   I don't want the nickname "Badger" anymore.

4,575.   ~~I don't wanna know.~~ (Changed mind, 4/13/92)

4,576.   I don't want to be mauled by anything.

4,577. I don't want to be on the losing side of anything that is called "the Trial of the Century."

4,578. I don't want the Lacerating Lioness to know how hot I think she is.

4,579. I don't want this bookcase anymore.

4,580. I don't want math to be right.

4,581. I don't want subscriptions to magazines I won't read.

4,582. I don't want to kill anything in vain (in vein and in vane are both okay).

4,583. I don't want to come back down from this cloud.

4,584. I don't want everything I've ever killed to come back alive because of a toxic chemical spill.

4,585. I don't want to talk about it.

4,586. I don't want to do this stupid show anymore.

4,587. I don't want those damn busybodies sticking their noses into my business.

4,588. I don't want my instincts to ever be wrong.

WEAPON HIGHLIGHT

KASURI-KAMA

This simple weighted chain and handheld sickle is also called the Farmer's Friend. It was originally used by livestock owners to defend against things that wanted to eat their cattle. Chupacabras, centipedes, fat people. All of them fell with bloody regret under the kasuri-kama.

The weapon has thousands of uses, limited only by your deadly imagination, but here are three favorite kasuri-kama techniques. For means of better illustration, let's say you are fighting an evil cow-munching fat person.

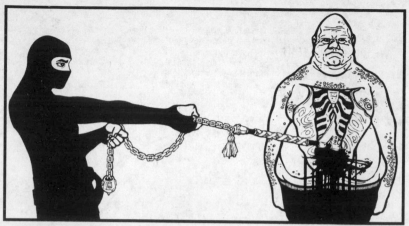

1. Whip the sickle around by the chain to build up speed and then sink it into the fat person and yank out something important.

2. Use chain to strangle, trip, or remove a weapon, while sickle gashes.

3. The Swinging Twins technique.

SAFE KASURI-KAMA USE

DO be careful when rolling up the chain. Getting a piece of skin caught in a chain link really stings.

DO build up speed when passing your kasuri-kama to another ninja.

DO develop quality praying mantis and toucan impressions with your weapon. They are very entertaining.

DO check the connection between the kasuri and the kama before each mission. You do not want that thing flying off . . . usually.

DO NOT use as just a kasuri or just a kama. That's what kasuris and kamas are for. This is a kasuri-kama.

DO NOT tle glow sticks to and take to a rave. It's tempting.

DO NOT use as a fruit or remote "grabber" at home. That's lazy.

DO NOT hesitate to attach the weapon to your tabi boot or elbow. That'll leave your hands free for holding other weapons or more kasuri-kamas.

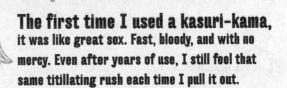

The first time I used a kasuri-kama, it was like great sex. Fast, bloody, and with no mercy. Even after years of use, I still feel that same titillating rush each time I pull it out.

—Randy the Spear, ninja

WARNING: Before weapon use, be sure to consult "Weapon Care and Training," page 275.

Opinjas: Woody Allen

Up till *Bullets over Broadway* he was great. After that, he should have been split stem to stern with a rusty hubcap.

—Perfect Storm, age 45

Man, I bet his nasty old ass has tagged Scarlett Johansson.

—R.I.P. Torn, age 18

He's hilarious. He's like a nebbishy, weak, untrained, Ninjew.

—Swart Dart, age 65

O-VER RA-TED (clap clap clap clap clap).

—Ooloo Bolo, age 346

The Curse of the Jade Scorpion is his *Citizen Kane.*

—Roger, age 30

I don't watch BET.

—Super Spit, age 93

What do you think?

_____

_____

RUMSPRINJA

You are nearing the end of the path. Many things about your life have changed, and there are many exciting and potentially incinerating ninja adventures waiting ahead for you. But are you *sure* you want to be this ninja that you set out to become? Do you have any doubts left in your mind that the ninja way you seek? If so, it is time for Rumsprinja.

Rumsprinja is a one-day return to your old life. Spend one full day doing all of the weak, pathetic, worthless things that used to occupy your time. Challenge yourself to really be as lame as you were before you started the path. Eat those greasy, processed, cheese things. Watch a ninja movie with enthusiasm and no trace of disdain. Apply for that "sweet" job that Mr. Weber thought would be "right up your alley." Cry yourself to sleep in a quivering mass of discomposure. Face the emptiness of your past and decide if it will define for you a crummy, wretched, desolate, irrelevant future.

WELL?

☐ I AM NINJA   ☐ i suck

The Bleeding Edge

Before trying to pass yourself off as a ninja, take a few seconds to assess and confirm your worthiness.

MASTER'S WRAP-UP

Meet with a ninja master in a crowded place full of non-ninjas. Have a pizza party without alerting a single person (skee-ball required).

CLANVERSATIONS

Discuss the following questions with your clanmates.

1. Who do you trust?

2. Who am I?

3. Is there good? Bad? Right? Wrong?

NINJA PROVERB

Few are the questions that cannot be answered with a well-placed foot.

—Asnap, ninja

SECTION III

The two halves of a wion fight over what type of baby to eat for dinner.

The You of Tomorrow

After stealing some tangerines from a coven of giant sea monkeys, the Ninja quizzes his apprentice on types of dragons.

If you've been *living* the book, by now you don't need to read this. You should be able to absorb information from written text with inksmosis.* If you're still reading this book, then you haven't been doing the exercises or living the way of the ninja.

If you're still reading, you may also want to start running, as there has probably been a ninja

---

* The free information flow between mind and page without the use of sight, sound, touch, or smaste.

dispatched to dispatch you. The running won't save you, but it's good exercise and no one wants to die fat.

For those of you absorbing this who have actually become I.T.A.N.'s, it's time to make the pursuit of true ninjaness your life. It is time for you to become known for being unknown, to kill that which most did not even know existed, much less needed to be killed, to finally use that thing with the chain and the stick and the knife* to do something besides grab snacks from the kitchen while you're in the backyard. The lore and knowledge in the remainder of this book is based on real ninja living and will help you in your lifelong pursuit.

It's time to do the ninja thing.

Where are the Aziza[†] of my laziness
Eaten by the Wion[‡] of my Sleipnir[§] spirit
Distant Fomorian[**] echoes of a flimsy Homonculus[††]
Crushed by the Marakihan[‡‡] of hard action

Merit Badges

Why would those who are not seen need marks of recognition for things that there is no trace of their ever doing? Good question. That's why real ninjas don't use merit badges. The merit badge system was created to (1) push practitioners beyond the

---

*Chickife.

[†] Really boring fairies.

[‡] Wolf lion, very cute, but very fierce and fairly conflicted.

[§] Powerful and magical eight-legged horse.

[**] A kind of Irish goatman that didn't last too long due to the combination of being Irish, a goat, and a man.

[††] Tiny man-made men made of bone, animal skin, and semen.

[‡‡] A giant man-headed fish that sucks in boats with its tubular tongue and squeezes them to bits.

capacity of their will and skill in the ninja things they do and (2) force practitioners to try new activities that make them vomit, faint, or lose control of their poophole. Think of a merit badge as an invitation* to explore† an exciting‡ ninja subject, a way of enticing you to fully probe the depth and intricacy of ninja training.

Why merit badges? Colored belts seemed childish and forearm brands from red-hot cauldron ceremonies were a scheduling nightmare and costing a fortune in rice paper. So it's merit badges.

The emblem on each badge shows that you have been tested by a master in a given skill and have lived to wear it. Many pursuers of the path have found deathlong hobbies or inspiration for great dark pledges of honor through their merit badge work. Sword master Charlie the Chopper testifies that his love of delimbing things started while angling for his Hacking and Whacking badge.

Merit advancement demands that you move at ninja speed. Rather than competing against others of equal skill, you have a master who will bring you great pain and dislocations if you do not progress at a rate that pleases him. Each distinction of darkness will be harder than herding coked-up fireflies at a rave.

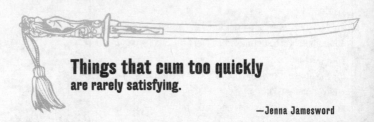

Things that cum too quickly
are rarely satisfying.

—Jenna Jamesword

---

* Order under the penalty of death.
† Survive under the penalty of death.
‡ Exciting includes dangerous, deadly, painful, maddening, and fun.

Fulfilling the blood oath you take before starting each merit badge is your burden alone. Although there are several badges that can or must be achieved with your clan, each member should feel a deep sense of severe, soul-gripping, Catholic-times-Jewish, guilt-like obligation that keeps their enthusiasm high.

You should carefully review all of the requirements before starting after a badge. The requirements for each badge are written on an unremovable scroll kept in the temple of Sharp Flying Objects. It is suggested that you duck a lot while reading over them.

Merit badges may be worn on a black merit badge swath that must be hidden at all times or tightly sewn to the inner leg beginning three inches above the ankle and ending no closer than one inch from the genitalia (on a warm day).

EARNING A MERIT BADGE

1. Retrieve the list of requirements by climbing to the Temple of Sharp Flying Objects, sneaking in past the Grave Lemurs and memorizing them from the Scroll of Worthiness.
2. Meet with a ninja master to fill out your merit badge application and to decide which ninja will harshly judge your attempt.
3. Complete the requirements under the eyes of no one and with no guidance or aid.
4. Face your merit arbiter and explain to him in rhyming verse what you have done to earn this ridiculous ornamentation. He will immediately know if you are telling the truth and either present you with a fun little patch or punish you mercilessly with wording and torture of his choosing.

MERIT BADGES REQUIRED FOR I.T.A.N.

OPENING

REMOVING

THROUGHING

The secret to saying something
is saying nothing.

—Killbox, ninja master

UNSEEN CITIZEN OF THE WORLD

DEATH AIDE

SCROLLING

Darkness is only scary
to those standing in the light.

—Tengu Whip, ninja master

DISORIENTEERING

MEDITATIONSHIP

NEEDLEPOINT

Minds are like parachutes, they stop
working when you poke a lot of holes in them.

—Sting, teacher

5,000-WEAPON CLUB

DRAGON GAUNTLET

BARE HANDS

Do not consider that anything
has been killed if anything is left to be killed.

—Snively Whiplash, ninja master

YOU KILLED MY MASTER

DEATHOGRAPHY

VOIDING

We think in generalities,
but we die in the details.

—Slade, ninja

SNAPPING

OUT OF NOWHERE

UNBELIEVABLE PAIN

When we all kill alike,
no one is killing very much.

—The Toll, ninja

BLACKWATER

MIMICRY

HARD-CORE SHIT

SECTION IV

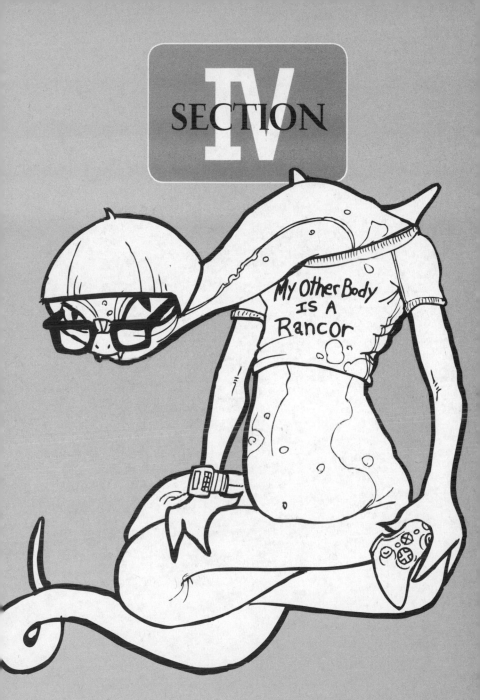

Although not physically imposing, the wingless nerd dragon can hack any social network and make you look like a total douche bag.

9

Jumping

This section attempts to cover
the most common full-body thrust, the jump.

Jumping is an art form and skill of the highest
difficulty. Please use this resource *only* as a cur-
sory overview of jumping and a good place to start.
For deeper study, please acquire the definitive

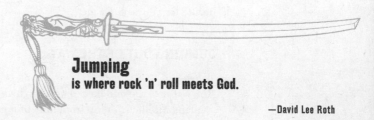

Jumping
is where rock 'n' roll meets God.

—David Lee Roth

collective on body thrusting, *Move It!* by David Lee Roth.

Have you ever heard the saying "Don't jump unless you know where you're going to land?" That is a stupid saying filled with fear of the unknown. Ninjas love the unknown, for it is in the unknown that the ninja has his most freedom. Take this as an encouragement as we wade into jumping.

There are five basic kinds of jumping.

KINDS OF JUMPING

1. Out of the Way

2. Into the Way (also called Jumping At)

3. On/In

4. Off

5. Around

To master the first two kinds of jumping, one must first understand what "the way" is. To the layman (or lameman) "the way" is anything he can see. Obviously, this isn't good enough for the ninja. For the ninja, the way includes anything your enemy can see, anything that anything your enemy can see can see, and anything that either of those will be able see before the ninja strikes again. Sounds pretty simple, huh? Try the following exercises and decide for yourself. Or die.

JUMPING OUT OF THE WAY

Warm-up
Run out into the middle of a busy highway at night wearing all black. Jump from lane to lane without getting hit.

Workout

STEP ONE: Wrangle a five-headed feral fairy. As you should know by now, they're constantly agitated, and not only can they look in five directions at once, but they can actually throw their eyeballs and still be able to see out of them.

STEP TWO: Go out into the center of the Gobi Desert and release your perturbed captive (for obvious reasons, you should not have physically touched the five-headed feral fairy in any way).

STEP THREE: Jump out of the way.

Since fairies can see through sand, you'll really have to focus your jump to land in or behind something that is made of either plastic or skin. Pretty tricky in the desert. Make sure you get it right on the first jump. If a feral fairy touches you, she will make you forget where you came from and where you are going.

JUMPING IN THE WAY

Jumping in the way is *not* the exact opposite of jumping out of the way. The key idea to remember here is that as you enter "the way" you still want to land in a position of balance and power. Basically, you don't want to jump into death. Jumping in the way is a time-honored technique used only by the bravest and most highly trained ninjas.

Warm-up

Dress in a fluorescent pink, skintight leotard and stand at the entrance to Costco on a Saturday morning. Using small, focused hops, jump into the way of everyone who tries to enter the superstore. (If you are already a fairly experienced jumper, try the same exercise at the entrance to Grand Central Station or a U2 concert.)

Workout

Obviously it would be quite silly to use a five-headed feral fairy to work on this technique. Instead, you will need a vampire.

> STEP ONE: Piss off a vampire. (Shouldn't be hard. Most of them have egos the size of Transylvania.)

> STEP TWO: Invite the ornery bloodsucker to a large, relatively empty room. High school gymnasiums or the floor of Congress work nicely.

> STEP THREE: Turn off all of the lights and jump in the way of the vampire's shadow. Vampires are one of the few creatures that only have shadows in the most pitch black. You will really have to focus your jump to land safely between the vampire and his shadow. Vampires are quick and have very finely tuned-in senses for the undead. Your goal is to land ready to fight the shadow, but completely undetected by the vampire.

JUMPING ON/IN

This is arguably the most difficult jumping style. More than in the way, in and on suggest that you are going to be making physical contact with an enemy during the jump. So, for starters, you definitely want to decide if you are aiming to jump in or on. On is a solid battle maneuver used to access elusive areas of vulnerability or avoid lava.

In is just plain messy.

Like all jumps you want to think about your landing. If you're jumping on a Cyclops to pull his eye out, you don't want to land on his forehead. Sure, it's a safe place to land on a Cyclops, but it will offer you no leverage when you swing your chigiriki* through his pupil. Similarly, if you're jump-

---

* A short bamboo reed with a heavy-duty chain and spiked ball attached. (No, it is not a mace. Geez.)

ing into a Cyclops to steal his golden pancreas, you want to make sure you jump all the way into his lungs so that you have the room you're going to need to wield your broadsword.

Try a few of these examples and keep the formula handy for the next time you need to jump in or on.

OBJECT: Shaquille O'Neal
ON/IN?: _____

GOAL: Remove Superman tattoo
WHERE TO LAND: _____

OBJECT: Possessed Skyscraper
ON/IN?: _____

GOAL: Rescue Sigourney Weaver
WHERE TO LAND: _____

OBJECT: Wingless Nerd Dragon
ON/IN?: _____

GOAL: Destroy giant inhaler
WHERE TO LAND: _____

OBJECT: Vermont
ON/IN?: _____

GOAL: To make finally die
WHERE TO LAND: _____

OBJECT: Sweaty Basilisk
ON/IN?: _____

GOAL: Detach 103rd vertebrae
WHERE TO LAND: _____

JUMPING OFF

Jumping off is the easiest of the jumps. It should and should not be taken lightly. Or should it?

The biggest mistake in jumping off is usually the choice of a jumping-off point. Points is a much better idea. You should always have at least five jumping-off points. One for each arm, one for each leg, and one for your head. Real ninjas on average have between 43 and 97 jumping-off points, depending on what they are on. Why so many points? Think about it: You're trying to get off something. There is probably a reason. It doesn't want you on it. Something else is about to jump on it. You've just placed an exploding emu in its ear. Whatever. You want off.

Having multiple jumping-off points gives you options. Let's say you're on the back of a turt-lantula.

Depending on the creature's movements, you can in an instant choose the best possible jumping-off point.

Apply the exact same theory of jumping-off points to your landing as well. Have options. You don't know what might change while you're in the air.

Jumping-off point: left butt check.

Jumping off point: pinkie finger.

Jumping-off point: tongue.

Landing in the Well of Souls.

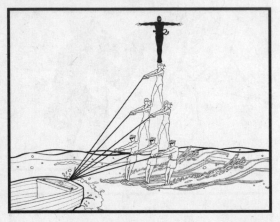

Landing on an average teen outing
(circa 1953).

Landing in the lamest party ever.

JUMPING AROUND

Jumping around is a rare but useful tool. It's also an extremely advanced technique that takes years of diligent training before even the mildest attempt can be made. There are no novice exercises or satisfactory single-panel illustrations to capture the intensity of jumping around. But for the purposes of general enlightenment, here are five of the main rules for jumping around.

1. HAVE A REASON. Jumping around takes a lot of energy.

2. DON'T JUMP AROUND LIKE AN IDIOT. Plan each jump as much as possible so that you don't look stupid.

3. JUMPING AROUND IS NOT JUST JUMPING UP AND DOWN. Diversify. If you are going to jump around, really jump all around.

4. DO NOT JUMP TO THE BEAT. An easy trap for rookies. Most beasts, except ogres, have a decent sense of rhythm. They will catch on and stick something through you on the downbeat.

5. MIX UP your jumping around with other random movements like scurrying, jolting, twisting, jamming, and flipping out.

Spinning

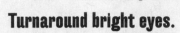

Turnaround bright eyes.

—Bonnie Tyler, "Total Eclipse
of the Heart"

The Babylonian king Hammurabi was known for saying, "One good turn deserves another." Ninjas feel that if the turn were good enough to begin with, you wouldn't need another one.

Unlike many ninja techniques, spinning is quite simple in concept and execution. At its core it basically involves turning around. It is essential, however, to master this technique in as many forms as possible. Why? Well, most simply because spinning, more than any other body movement, is almost always used in *conjunction* with another body movement. For example, a spin-kick involves a spin *and* a kick. Of course, you must also consider what type of spin is best for this kick and for the thing being kicked. You don't want to be pondering these questions in the heat of battle. That is why you must master the spin until it is instinct . . . and then practice a little bit more until it is ninstinct.

KINDS OF SPINNING

1. Around
   - Fast
   - Slow

2. In the wind

3. On a dime

4. Like a top

SPINNING AROUND

Spinning around is the cornerstone of all turning. If you can't master it you might as well just not turn around and go home.

No doubt you have turned around before, but you've probably done so without thought, at a moderate speed, and under the direction of someone else. Never with the sense of purpose and focus in which a ninja does things.

Spin around.

You're just staring at this page aren't you? You're trying to figure out if I meant 180 degrees or 360 degress.

The reality is neither. You have been brainwashed with limitations. You should *never* spin as someone else tells you to. It is *your* body that is turning. It should rotate only as far as you decide. This idea is called "owning your spin."

Let's look at the two ninja forms of spinning around: fast and slow.

Spinning around fast is as common to a ninja as breaking bones. It should feel natural and completely under your control. Rule number one in turning is never spin out of control. Giving up or giving over control of your spin is like giving up control of your knee. Do you want someone or something else to decide which way and how far your knee should turn?

This game played by ninja children will provide a useful beginner's exercise. It is simple and super-fun, but also great for building up your control and consciousness of your fast spin around.

The game is called Baby Catch.

Stand in a pitch-black room and get your bearings.

ROUND ONE: Throw a baby up in the air.

Spin around three times and catch the baby.

ROUND TWO: Throw a baby in the air and poke a black adder with a stick.

Spin around four times. Kill the snake. Catch the baby.

ROUND THREE: Throw a baby, poke an adder, and press the button on the remote crossbow aimed at your head.

Spin around five times. Shatter arrow. Kill snake. Catch baby.

ROUND FOUR: Throw baby, poke snake, shoot arrow, and press send on a regrettable e-mail to an ex-lover.

Spin around six times. Unplug the computer. Shatter arrow. Kill snake. Catch baby.

ROUND FIVE: Throw baby, poke snake, shoot arrow, send regrettable e-mail, and kick a nest of killer hornets.

Spin around seven times. Strangle each hornet. Unplug computer. Shatter arrow. Kill snake. Catch baby.

As you can see, the game is virtually endless. For each round just add a new challenge *and* another spin. You must handle the challenges in the exact reverse order in which you instigate them.

This game is also a great den activity to play every month. Make it a friendly competition to see who can get to the highest round before missing the baby.

Now let's look at spinning around slow. Nope, that is not a typo. Slow. Believe it or not, this is a ninja move. A vital one. Yes, ninjas are fast. Some of 'em are real fast. But of all the beings you will fight, ninjas are not the fastest. And when you're facing something faster than you, slowing down actually serves as a better tactical move.

A fearbot fly* weighs only $4\frac{1}{2}$ pounds and is unable to hold any weapons, yet it has been responsible for the deaths of thousands of Killersapiens. Why? Because it's fast. Damn fast. So damn fast in fact that it can fly through solid objects (i.e., people). You can spin till your heart's content, but you will never spin faster than a fearbot fly.

Several hundred years ago, a fearbot fly landed behind a ninja master named Doowha. Doowha stayed perfectly still and began to study the benefits of slowing down. Three months later, to the complete surprise of the fearbot fly, Master Doowha was facing the fly and driving a dagger through its back.

Since it would be silly, and mostly likely deadly, to practice your slow-turning technique on something faster than yourself, try using regular people. Here is a time-consuming but time-tested Slow Spin Around exercise.

1. Replace a life-sized statue in a high-traffic and popular tourist location with yourself dressed as that statue.

2. Keep a constant, extremely slow spin going for one solid month.

If any one notices you turning, kill him or her and start again.

SPINNING IN THE WIND

Spinning in the wind—or twisting in the wind, as it is often incorrectly referred to—is the most complicated and dangerous spinning maneuver. Wind cannot be trusted. It is as fickle and tem-

* A large robotic burrowing fly that is programmed to move 50 percent faster than its opponent.

peramental as Julia Roberts. You cannot tell the wind what to do. Your only option is to listen for its subtle clues. This is difficult, since wind may be the one thing sneakier than a ninja. Wind also has an amazing range of power. It can kiss the cheek of a newborn mouse or pick up a house and crush a newborn mouse. Another thing to consider when spinning in the wind is that you are in midair with no "solid" surface to ground your axis of spin. Therefore, this spinning technique involves perpetually changing direction and overall orientation.

I have never seen any space more underused than air.

—Twiggy, 1960s model

If you plan on using wind to attack a castle from above or battle a hippogryph in flight or get away for the weekend, you best get wind spinning down cold.

You may be wondering, "Why do I have to spin in the wind? Why can't I just float? Or drift?" Quite honestly, that is some pretty stupid wondering. The answer is that wind is in eternal motion, and you have to stay in an unceasing spin to keep in touch with what the wind is up to. It's like friends in high school. If you lose touch with them for even one summer, they will instantly transform into some sort of extreme weirdo who only listens to bands from Iceland or says "braugh" way too much or has really bad acne. You have to expose every cell and nerve ending possible to the surrounding air movement so that your body can react at the speed of the wind.

Dancing Leaves.

Mountain Storm.

Titty Twister.

There is no practice exercise for actual wind spinning. It's a sink-or-swim situation—or rather fly or fall. (Of course, you are not actually flying. Flying implies that you have much more control over your air passage than spinning will allow you.)

But there are a few things you can do to prepare.

·Strip naked and climb to the top of a flagpole. Stand on the little ball at the top and really feel the wind around you. Listen to it. The wind will talk to you. Not about your favorite breakfast cereal or whether or not you like the new Olsen Twins' project, but rather about how it is moving.

·Double-check your flexibility. You have to be able to move everything everywhere in order to wind spin successfully. At minimum make sure you can

- Touch each ear with each toe.
- Bend over backward so that your ankles can massage your temples.
- Sit so cross-legged that each knee can touch the outside of the opposite hip.

·Think lightly. There is nothing that will drop you out of the clouds faster than heavy thoughts. While wind spinning one day, a very talented ninja could not contain his brain from thinking about how absolute zero was illogically conceived based on the three-dimensional existence of atoms. He plummeted like a refrigerator and broke his heart.

If you have prepared to the best of your ability, there is but one thing left to do. Go jump off a cliff.

SPINNING ON A DIME

Spinning on a dime is the technique by which you change directions quickly while at full speed without breaking stride.

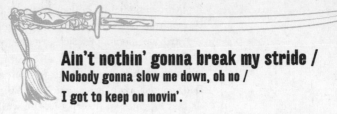

Ain't nothin' gonna break my stride /
Nobody gonna slow me down, oh no /
I got to keep on movin'.

—Matthew Wilder, "Break My Stride"

LESSON IN LITERATURE:
THERE'S NO M IN CHOP, BY ADMIRAL YAMAMOTO

Ri Gyokko was a beautiful ninja raised in the snowy northern mountains of India. It is said that she could stop an avalanche by winking at it. One day while chopping pines trees into paper with her bare hands, she heard the cry of her beloved dog Old Shusher. Ri began to run at full speed toward the sound. It appeared to be coming from her cave. She ran headfirst into the cave. At the last moment, as her eyes adjusted to the darkness she realized it was not her beloved canine at all. It was an immense snowagator with its mouth open mimicking Old Shusher. Ri spun on a dime and hightailed it out of there before the arctic reptile could snap shut its 80-gallon mouth.

In the rest of the story, we find out that Ri does go back and kill the snowagator. She makes a sweater for Old Shusher from the skin and enough gator-jerky to last her through the winter. But if Ri had not been able to spin on a dime, it would have been the extremely cold-blooded predator that would have been making sweaters and jerky out of her.

No matter how ultimate you are as a ninja, there are still going to be times when you need to change direction while at top speeds. Sometimes it will be turning around from a moose that you suddenly realize has a cobra for a tongue. It may also be spinning back around on a gorebore that you've lured out of its tree by tying lemons to your back. Maybe you need to catch a clown, but he's throwing deadly balloon animals at you. All of those situations would involve spinning on a dime.

Hard work and practice are the only ways to master this spin.

Paint a white line 1 meter in front of an electrified, spiked metal wall. Back up 20 meters. Run as fast as you can directly at the wall. When you reach the white line, instantly turn without slowing down. As you repeat, continue to move the white line closer and closer to the electrified, spiked steel wall. When you can get within 17.91 millimeters (the diameter of a dime), you have reached ninja mastery of this skill.

SPINNING LIKE A TOP

The quality of a spin is, of course, the most important component, but quantity is also important. Think about all the things in your life that can't be handled with just one. Just one keystroke won't work for a court reporter. You can't win a baseball game by throwing only one pitch. Neither participant gets much satisfaction out of one thrust of a penis into a vagina. The same goes for spins. How many spins will exactly be needed, one never knows, but one should be prepared for as many as are necessary.

Seemingly, the logical way to practice spinning around multiple times is simply to spin around multiple times. Unfortunately, this is also boring and pretty stupid looking.

So let's dance. Break-dance, to be exact.

Break dancing was an art form developed by ninjas to express themselves socially while displaying the astonishing skills they had mastered. The "toplike" spin is integral to the rhythmic communication of those skills.

The following grid was donated by the Get Fresh Clan after a rousing spin-off with rival clan Panther Punch Posse in the garage of Julian Cashman (a.k.a. Ju-Cash-2) and DJ'd by Slize So Nize.

- Gather your den together in a circle around a large, flat piece of cardboard or linoleum.

- Get a beat going. Make your own or hire a DJ to drop mad science on the scene.

- Take turns stepping up and spinning it out in the middle.

- Use a grid to mark down who gets the most spins for each body part.

SPIN	SPINNER	# OF SPINS
Back	Dope Dragon	50,486
Head	Blud Brotha	72,002
Knee	Kutchu	6,378
Ankle	Snap Dogg	9,528
Kidney	Deth Breth	45
Shoulder	RadiKill	20,890
Calf	Die Job	10,672
Nose	Star Wype	2,000
Tongue	Cuttilynguist	5,321
Nipple	Punk Sure U	987
Uvula	Trip N Stab	1,053
Penis	D-Bone-R	12

Nose spin.

Kicking

Kick it!

—Ad-Rock, "Fight for Your Right to Party"

This is it, folks. The original ninja move. The kick predates every ninja technique, even the punch. It is considered the most important and revered fighting maneuver. Some of the ancient masters spent their entire lives perfecting and training in the Legged Arts.

Each year, the Ninja Society for Activity Below the Waist puts out a comprehensive encyclopedia of kicks. But no words can ever seem to capture the pure joy and childlike wonder of swinging your leg at someone.

There are over 6,000 specifically defined and designed kicks used by ninjas today. In a recent article in *Bruiseweek* magazine, 15 blind grand masters were asked to create a list of the 100 most influential ninja kicks. The list got finished, but only 3 of the blind grand masters are still alive.

1. Kick of 1,000 Cracks

2. Judith Lights-Out Kick

3. Golden Foot Bath

4. Woe Is Knee Kick

5. Smash Mouth

6. Red Ankle of Sleep

7. Diecycle Kick

8. Didn't You Used to Have a Head Kick

9. 10 Piggies of Pain

10. The Flying Life Insurance Payout

11. Revolving Foot Introduction

12. The Mongolian Metatarsal Parcel

13. Here's the Kicker Kick

14. Step Class of Misery

15. The Spinning Shark Leg

16. The Dragon De-Winger

17. Lungopop Kick

Second Half Kickoff

18. Your Ass Kick

19. Flaming Toe Jam

20. Highway to Heel

•Judith Lights-Out Kick. This is a highly controlled kick that involves much forethought and planning. You must first lure a hunky Italian into your home and gain his trust. Then you sneak into his room late at night while he is sleeping and kick him so hard that when he wakes up, he's in love with you.

21. Fatal-Foot Funk Kick

22. Exit Stage Death

23. Mongoose Power Trip

24. The Butler

25. Terminating Toe Knee Tiger Kick

26. The Supreme Shin of Silence

27. W.T.F. Kick

28. Arch of Annihilation

29. Foot in Mouth Decease

30. System of a Down

31. The Bucket Kick

32. Club Foot Sandwich

33. Corns of Chaos

34. Toenado Kick

35. The Lead-Foot Driving Kick

36. The Naughty Sock Puppet

37. Unauthorized Surgery

38. Around the World in Achy Daze

39. The Long Kick Goodnight

40. Second Half Kickoff

Run Knee Nose Crush

•The Butler. Very widely used powerful kick of death developed in the late 1800s. You attend an upscale mansion party disguised as a servant. At a strategic moment, you cut the lights, kick your intended mark to death, and disappear before the lights come on.

•**Second Half Kickoff.** A ninja usually builds up some speed by running about 10 yards before delivering a forceful, precise blow to the waist, literally knocking the lower half of the victim's body off of his person. There is, of course, a sister kick to this one for the first half.

41. The Dream Cleaver (must be done while enemy is sleeping)

42. The Feral Frank Footer

43. Eat My Feet

44. Brain Pong

45. The Not-So-Soft Shoe

46. Forty-Odd Feet of Grunts

47. Mr. Belvedere's Dropkick

48. Butter Churn of Death

49. GOAL!

50. Just Four Kicks

51. Roadhouse Roundhouse

52. Triple Chicken Leg Sweep

The Habit Kick

53. I Kneed You Tonight

54. Instant Regret

55. Agony of Da Feet

56. I Get a Kick in to You

57. Master Morty's Bludgeoning Bunyun

58. The Melting Hot Foot

59. The Underwater Flipper Flap

60. Driving Miss Daisy

•**Just Four Kicks.** As the name implies, there are actually four kicks that make up this move. Each of the kicks carries the weight of universal righteousness. It is primarily used on evil undead-like vampires and demons like kangaroos. The four kicks are the Kick of Justice, the Kick of Think About What You've Done, the Kick of It Doesn't Sound Like You're Sorry, and the Kick of I Believe You But I'm Not Ready to Trust You Again Yet.

61. Leg Peg

62. The Four Lions of Foot Town

63. The Bladed Moonwalk

64. Cause and a Foot

65. The Saget Worthy Groin Kick

66. Thigh-high Bye-Bye

67. Underneath Sheet Kick

68. Double-Sided Curtains

69. The Wrongest Foot

70. Whoa Whoa Woe Kick

71. The Habit Kick

72. The Foot Locker

73. Kicking Down the Avenue

74. W00t B00t

75. The Iron Whammy Bar

76. Thunderbolting Lightfoot

77. The Hungarian Hip Remover

78. Now You See It Now You're Dead

79. The Superhero Sidekick

80. The Barbarous Boot of Bedlam

•**The Habit Kick.** This is a very positive philanthropic kick developed by a team of Smackback Monkeys. The delivery of this blow can actually kick the addiction of any substance right out of a body.

81. Two Feet Deep Kick

82. The Considerate Canadian Kick

83. Blanda's Revenge

84. The Kick of Destiny

85. The Urban Curbin'

86. Jaws IV

87. The Pungent Sole Patch

88. The Unbelievable Snake Kick

89. The Stomp Tour

90. The Yakuza Kickback

91. The Sweaty Ax

92. Kicks Incorporated

93. The Single Maker

The Considerate Canadian Kick

94. A Kick Before Dying

95. Reverse Back Side Front Kick

96. Palace of Endless Toes

97. Kick of the Savage Butterfly

98. Curse of the Callus

99. Run Knee Nose Crush

100. Somebody Watch Where That Thing Lands

•The Considerate Canadian Kick. This is by far the softest ninja kick. It is designed to merely make your opponent aware that you're somewhat distressed at his behavior, but that you're keeping all channels of communication open. It is mostly used on Mainers and other dim creatures.

Punching

The punch—or "handed kick," as it was originally known—is a fascinating and diverse strike. The arms and hands used for punching are (on average) half as strong but twice as mobile as the legs and feet used for kicking. This makes the punch tremendously useful, although not as powerful as the kick.

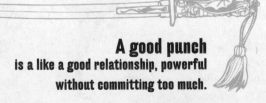

A good punch
is a like a good relationship, powerful
without committing too much.

—Twisted Fister, ninja

Certainly by now you have heard of the concepts of Wind, Fire, Water, and Earth. All fighting styles separate these elements into four isolated techniques, except for the ninja. This is why a ninja punch will automatically be four times more powerful than any other punch right from the get-go.

WIND: Light and Fast, like a ninja or a pretheater dinner.

FIRE: Erratic and Painful, like a ninja or high school talent show auditions.

WATER: Malleable and Smooth, like a ninja or fruit punch.

EARTH: Hard and Rough, like a ninja or giving a coherent, logical explanation for what she is doing here.

A ninja punch must be all of these things.

Although every ninja punch combines the four elements of fighting, ninja punches do fall in to three punching categories.

AHNTU

The Ahntu style consists of any blow or combination of blows meant to strike the surface of an adversary. These are attention-getters that may or may not be lethal. Popular punches in this class include the Arm of Harm, the Five Finger Dis, and the Bitch Slap.

Many Ahntu punches involve more than one strike. The Arm of Harm, for example, incorporates a fist smash, an elbow jab, and a shoulder knock. Even though the whole punch takes less than one second, thanks to stop-motion drawing we can look at the effects of each phase of the Arm of Harm on an extremely deadly foe.

The Lung-eating Witch of Vileville faces a ninja about to use the Arm of Harm.

Fist smash.

Followed by an elbow jab.

Finished with a shoulder knock.

ENTU

An ancient ninja master realized one day whilst fighting a chimera that punching his fist and arm *into* the beasts and removing things aided him in defeating his foes. Thus was born the Entu punching style. The style involves inserting part or all of the punching apparatus inside the foe and mangling or extracting vital regions. Some of the popular Entu punches among ninjas are the Knuckle Sandwich (into the mouth), the Hand Job (into the hand), and Operate! (into the torso).

It's important to really know the anatomy of your adversary before you reach inside of them. You need to know what you're grabbing, how to detach it, and where/how deep it is. If you plunge into a chichevache* intending to yank out a heart and you end up holding a "still beating" stomach in front of his face, you are gonna feel pretty foolish. They have four of 'em.

Again using our wretched, demonic foe, let's take a look at a properly executed Operate! punch.

---

* Eternally starved cow that can change its face to look like any out-of-work actor.

The Lung-eating Witch of Vileville faces a ninja about to use an Operate! punch.

THARU

There are many times when a ninja is fighting multiple foes or has multiple missions to accomplish in a short span of time. These are the times when a Tharu punch* is most useful. Tharu punching is the challenging task of having the punch go in one side and out the other of whatever is being punched. Although difficult to master, it is the most economical and practical punch in a ninja's arsenal. In a recent slayer survey, it was revealed that 43 percent of all ninja punches go through (not just into) their foes.

The Tharu punch can either come in a chopping form, when aiming to remove body parts, or in stabbing motions, when either removing body parts or causing massive carnal damage. On the following pages are four pictures illustrating some of the most popular Tharu punches.

* Named after Hacky David Tharu, renowned puncher.

The Lung-eating Witch of Vileville faces a ninja about to use a Tharu punch.

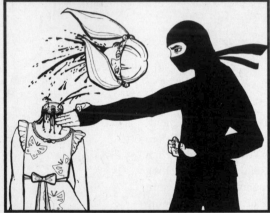

Slice of Heaven.

My Keys Are Behind You.

No Knee to Thank Me.

The previous examples were for illustrating technique and form. In an actual engagement, an adversary will rarely just stand there and let you beat the crap out of them.

Now, there is a fourth type of punch that has not been mentioned until now: the Kunch. It has not been mentioned because it is not really a punch. A Kunch is a fake punch followed by a real kick. Since a kick has the ability to deliver more force, the adversary is caught off-guard. No, there is no such thing as a fake kick/real punch because then you'd be delivering something softer than expected, and that is not the ninja way.

Ducking/Dodging

So you got to dodge 'im
and you got to duck 'im, /
You got to keep that diesel truckin'.

—Jerry Reed, "Eastbound and Down"

This skill is about one thing and one thing alone: getting the heck out of the way. You're not going to be able to punch and kick and stab if you've just been hit in the head with a bear-bone spear or bitten in half by a Bone Bear or crushed by a statue of DeForest Kelley naked.

"Look out!" and "Heads up" are not part of a ninja's vocabulary because they are never needed. We use all of our senses, not just our eyes, and move our bodies appropriately according to what we perceive. Even when a ninja is hidden, he is prepared to move if something accidentally comes at him. Because ducking and dodging require immediate access to all senses, it is quite dangerous to get the brain involved by discussing it in theory. A wise woman once said:

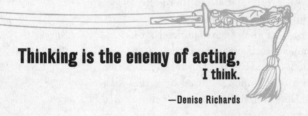

Thinking is the enemy of acting,
I think.

—Denise Richards

So without thinking, get up and go do the following exercises. It is suggested that you be naked the first time you do each exercise in order to build up your ability to sense all that is around you.

Warm-up
Go to your local batting cages and rent the fast-pitch cage for an hour. Empty the baseballs out of the pitching machine and fill it up with shurikens. Stand blindfolded on the little rubber home plate, start the machine, and don't get hit.

Exercise One
Although nature is an ally of the ninja, it is still quite unpredictable. Especially when it begins to

combine multiple forces. Multiple forces against multiple senses is a fair battle, and what this first exercise is all about.

Find yourself a nice hearty blizzard. Make sure it's at least five miles wide. Run through the blizzard without a single flake of snow touching you

Exercise Two

Let's turn it up a notch. Repeat exercise one, but replace the hearty blizzard with a sandstorm full of bedlambs.*

Exercise Three

For one month, simultaneously date a vampiress, an Amazonian queen, a mermaid, a witch, and a Hollywood actress. Tell each one that you love her and her alone, keeping each relationship hidden from the others. On the last day of the month, send the following e-mail to all of them.

> Dear Stinky Butt,
>
> I hate your face. I have totally been doing it with like all these models and sick people since the day we met. Consider this trash day and yous on the curb, biznatch.
>
> Eat Gerbil Poop, (her pet name for you)

Now dodge these scorned ladies and duck the hell that their crazy asses bring at you. You are not allowed to fight them or harm them in any way. You are only allowed to evade their fury. They did

---

* Rabid flying lambs that refuse to follow anyone or anything.

nothing wrong. You brought this upon yourself to better yourself as a ninja.

After six months, send the following e-mail to smooth things over and end the exercise.

```
Dear [Her real name],

My bad. You're the tops. Consider this
friend day, and you're mine.


☺ [Her pet name for you]
```

Crawl, Walk, Run

A few times I've been around
that track / So it's not just gonna happen like that.

—Gwen Stefani, "Hollaback Girl"

The ninja has the ability to mimic the movement of 87 percent of known creatures. Whether it is the whole body of a galloping leucrota* or moving as one horn of a nasty mantygre,† ninjas are masters of action impersonation.

---

* A dog-wolf with impossibly strong teeth and the fastest digestion system of any known carnivore.
† Tiger body, dragon feet, ox horns, and the head of a senile old man. Notoriously horrible dinner guests.

After slaying Barbara Walters
for her plot to implant a remote-control crying device into each newborn baby, I realized the zombie I had trained to replace her had just jumped out the window chasing one of Barbara's front teeth. Although I am 6'6" and 265 pounds, I spent the next six weeks moving among her closest friends as her until a new, more focused zombie could be trained.

—Dark Corner, ninja

There are, however, core ways of moving that are most commonly used by ninjas for transporting themselves. These walks are the carrot, the celery, and the onion base from which the soup of movement is made. The first mode of motion is the crawl.

THREE CRAWLS OF THE NINJA

1. **SNEAKAPEDE.** The lowest of all ninja movements. Lie flat on your stomach on the ground. Slide your body hair through your gui and use it to lift yourself up one centimeter off the ground. Now use your body hair like thousands of tiny legs to move you in any direction in a serpentine fashion.

2. **OSCILLATING OCTOPUS.** Another low technique that allows for increased mobility and is great if being chased. Throw 8 or 12 suction cups on your gui and drop flat on the ground. Recite the Secret Waterbone Incantation. You will become a loose mass of muscle (with suction cups) that moves about as you please.

3.   **RENEGADE INFANT.** Any limb-driven scurrying done below one-third of your height falls into this category. Make sure, like a baby, you only move when people are not looking.

THREE WALKS OF THE NINJA

1.   **SNEAKY SNEAK.** Hunch over while extending your arms palm down at waist level. Step forward, placing your weight only on your tippy toes. Creep forward in a gentle loping motion. Make a careful effort not to think of any plinking piano music that would nicely complement the walk.

2.   **CRAZY LEGS.** Loosen your hip, knee, ankle, and toe joints so that they have 270-degree mobility (do not loosen them to 360 degrees or you will lose control). As you try to walk normally, your body will naturally be pulled in all sorts of wacky directions. This is a perfect walk for approaching someone in plain view or moving through an area with snipers or multiheaded beasts.

3.   **INVISIBLE FOOT.** For this walking system, a ninja simply moves his legs so slowly that it is impossible to detect motion. A famous ninja named Crunky Bruiseter once used this walking method to get close enough to kill an Argus Panoptes* after challenging him to a game of red light/green light.

THREE RUNS OF THE NINJA

1.   **SHADOW RUN.** This highly technical run is the most popular ninja nighttime movement. It quite literally involves running in the cover

* An African giant with 100 eyes and an ego the size of Africa.

of shadows. A ninja must be keenly adept not only at seeing the next shadow, but also at knowing how to hide his body in it. One must run *in* the shadows of the night and not with them.

2.   **RUNNING STANDING STILL.** Run with a normal posture and relaxed breathing, but move your legs 1,000 times faster than normal. Your legs will be moving so fast that they will look like they are barely moving. Your enemy is sure to be surprised when you end up in his face a thousand times faster than he anticipated.

3.   **RUN OF THE MAGIC PANTHER ON FIRE.** This run has a slightly misleading name, as actually any of the big cats will do the trick so long as they are enchanted with a blaze spell. This run works by lighting the leopard, jaguar, panther, etc., on fire and aiming it toward your destination. You then run near the enkindled kitty, mimicking its four-legged style. Any enemy will dismiss you as a shadow cast by the ignited feline.

Stabbing/Slicing

Stabbing and slicing are straightforward enough.

STABBING: Sticking something through something.

SLICING: Drawing something across something, so that part of that second something is cleaved.

You'd be hard-pressed to find a ninja that doesn't stab and slice something at least once a day. By now on your journey, you should have stabbed and sliced many things. But did you stab and slice them *like a ninja?*

Before you read the below rules of cut, please understand three things: (1) Things change. An elf may be helping you move one day and be demonically possessed the next. (2) Not everything dies. If it doesn't, your job is to make it as not alive as possible. (3) There is an exception to every rule. There have been reports of goblins with three hearts, changelings that didn't change, and even Irishmen who weren't slobbering, fall-down drunks.

That being stated, the following are good *general* rules of cut.

OPPONENT	DESCRIPTION	STAB	SLICE
REGULAR	They are what they are.	Through major life points.	Off or through major life points.
LIVING DEAD	These things are already dead on at least one level, but are pretending they are still alive.	In the head.	Right between the living part and the dead part. Got to get them two parts separated.
UNDEAD	They should really be called Can't Dead. Whatever deal they have made, they cannot be killed.	Through the thickest part and to something very sturdy. Basically, this stab is trying to hold them still while you slice.	Up into as many tiny bits as possible. Whatever it is will still be alive, but you can spread the pieces all over the place and give it a bitch of a time re-forming itself
POSSESSED	Somebody else is controlling them. This is a risky, mixed bag of crazy.	The person that is controlling them. You have to remember the possessed thing is most likely not acting of its own will, and ninjas don't stab innocent people.	To incapacitate but not kill. Tendons and minor arteries are good choices.
ENCHANTED	There is a spell, charm, or incantation that magically protects or enhances part or all of their being.	The magic part, but make sure you have a sword that can withstand the sorcery that chaperones the creature. Magic loves making people look stupid.	Around the creature, making as many different items as possible fall in its path or strike it. This is called "bothering" and can often confuse and disorient the enchanted.
ETHEREAL	Have limited if any form and often span more than one realm or plane of existence.	Till your heart's content. You ain't hitting nothing. Don't even try. In millions of years of trying, no one has been able to stab one of these suckers.	Using a fan made from the antithesis of its celestial consciousness. Also, sometimes a really strong vacuum does the trick.

Know your opponent's anatomy. A troll's heart and brain are not in its chest and head.

You can stab and slice with one move. This ninja sliced the demonized horn of this evil unicorn in the same move with which he stabbed his sword through the evil brain and evil throat.

A good ninja always has plenty of extra stabby and slicey things on hand. Many blades makes light work.

Now draw in how you would stab and slice the following nefarious adversaries.

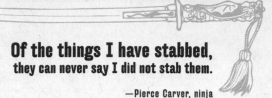

Of the things I have stabbed,
they can never say I did not stab them.

—Pierce Carver, ninja

Strangling/Choking

Many people think that strangling and choking are the same thing. Those people deserve to be choked and strangled. The two skills are as different as chocolate pudding and chocolate mousse.

Strangling is a killing move. It involves both pulmonary and respiratory assault and requires a physical interaction or tethering.

Choking is a respiratory assault only. It can be fatal, but death is not required, nor is any physical contact.

STRANGLING

Strangling is a thinking man's game. You really have to know your foe before engaging in this endeavor. Whether using your bare hands or a 12-foot manrikigusari, you are going to somehow be attached and/or tethered to the stranglee. If this is the case, you better be darn certain you know where the blood center and air processor are in relation to the thinking core. The human is easy. Evenly applied pressure around the neck cuts off blood flow and air to the brain. The jelly imp, however, is an achromatic beast of a different color. It's a gelatinous clear shape-shifter. Try throwing on a gold bikini and pulling a chain around that.

In order for a ninja to get his basic Strangling Badge, he must complete a Baneful Bog Beast strangling course. Each bog-dwelling monstrosity listed below has a unique placement(s) for its vital

areas of air and blood. Have a buddy mark off each
of the random and horrendous creatures as you
throttle the life out of them.

BANEFUL BOG BEAST STRANGLING COURSE (BASIC)

1. _____ Chiang-Shih (or Hopping Corpse). *Hint: This essence-sucking zombie is already dead. Whatcha gonna strangle?*

2. _____ Mud Golem. *Hint: It's tough to find the throat of wet dirt.*

3. _____ Spear-Headed Squirrel. *Hint: This sucker's a flesh burrower. You'd better find his vitals before he finds yours.*

4. _____ Bog Bear. *Hint: The only boneless bear that also has gills.*

5. _____ Selkie. *Hint: Seal? Person? Person? Seal? It may change midstrangle.*

6. _____ Feral Will. *Hint: What happens to all of your unmade choices when you die? Ask this 6'6" curly haired demon. He is no joke with no throat.*

7. _____ Flat Cat. *Hint: You have to find nine different ways to strangle this paper-thin feline.*

8. _____ Incubus. *Hint: The only way to draw him out is in your dreams. You literally have to strangle this bugger in your sleep.*

9. _____ Merror. *Hint: Even though this is an archfiend of possessed water, it is still distressing to kill an exact replica of yourself.*

10. _____ Wendigo Malice. *Hint: Not to be confused with Wendie Malick. Both are malevolent cannibalistic spirits, but only this one lives in a bog.*

CHOKING

Choking is always fun, but it can be dangerous if you don't follow a few key basic rules. The subtlety and effectiveness of the art form are easily lost if the practitioner is overconfident or underprepared.

Can you match the correct choking tool or technique with the right adversary?

CHOKER	CHOKEE
Bat Whip	Hag
Expanding Corsage	Scorpion Men
An Off-Color Joke	Leprecan't
High-Powered Drill (⅛ bit)	Prom Dragon
Bon Jovi CD	Mummies
Ass-Flavored Balloons	Ahool
Hippopotamus Urine	Jersey Devil
Regret	Republicans
Hemp Smoke	Each Uisge
White Dove	Evil Clown

ANSWER KEY: Bat Whip—Each Uisge; Expanding Corsage—Prom Dragon; An Off-Color Joke—Republicans; High-Powered Drill (⅛ bit)—Hag; Bon Jovi CD—Jersey Devil; Ass-Flavored Balloons—Ahool; Hippopotamus Urine—Scorpion Men; Regret—Mummies; Hemp Smoke—Evil Clown; White Dove—Leprecan't

Confusion and Distraction

Confusion and distraction are two of the most powerful weaponiques* because they are inside the mind of the enemy. That is to say, the ninja, who is physically outside of the mind of the enemy (at

* A combination of a weapon and a technique for using that weapon.

least usually), is accessing and manipulating an enemy's attention using these skillaments.* Please make a note that the mind is not the same thing as the brain. Brains can be accessed quite easily with cracking and scooping. A mind must be controlled with coercion and understanding.

A ninja always aims for confusion since it is much more powerful than simple distraction. In fact, distraction is often called the Ringo Starr of confusion—important but not all that good looking or interesting.

Applying confusion and/or distraction to a situation takes subtlety and precision. You must always make sure that you yourself don't get confused or distracted while attempting to confuse and distract. There was once a ninja who acted like a crazy person to distract a spug yeti.† He acted so well that he convinced himself that he was crazy. Now he *is* crazy. Another ninja tried to tell an adaro‡ a

---

* See *Weaponique*.
† A wampa-sized, tenacious furry beast that spits poisonous puppies. You see a puppy flying and you feel it would be cruel not to catch it . . . Bam, you're dead.
‡ Evil merman, smells fishy.

THE CHOKE LIST

1. Always assume that what you are choking is *not* going to choke to death.
2. Don't choke things that don't breathe.
3. Making something metaphorically choke is often better than actually choking it.
4. Train yourself to be able to detect the fake choke because that's when they tend to throw dirt or sand in your face.
5. Bring your choking materials with you. Do not expect the exact right thing to just magically be there.

riddle that made no sense. The ninja became so turned around and confused that he stabbed himself in the nose.

It is said that randomness is the fork nah-nah poopie pants LEFT! That doesn't make any sense, just like trying to confuse and distract something without having the proper skillaments at your disposal. Since you never know when you may need them, you must prepare your mind to conjure up the necessary weaponiques when needed. Every ninja should know the tools of distraction and the concepts of confusion. Below is a short starter list of some of the general ideas that help foster confusion and distraction. If this is your first time reading the list, you may want to examine it in small chunks (say, four or five at time) to avoid confusion.

Questions
Blue-green
The Forth Dimension
Under There
Rocks
100%
Wigs For Babies
The career of Miley Ray Cyrus
Pauses
Dark matter
Yelling
YouTube
Nothing
The end of *Superman Returns,* when he's in the kid's room
Gossip
Craisins®
Irony
Circus folk
Pain
Nougat
Women
Food that advertises eating it
Getting hit in the groin
Time
Overdone

Scattered valuables
Any word of eight letters or more that's all vowels
Body temperature
Boobs
Puns (not double entendre)
Buttons
Where you go when you read
Art
Three
Political action committees
Possibility
Coolness
Explosions
Blue food
Surprises
Motives
Finger licking/sucking
Religion
Dance crazes
Reality
Shiny things
The difference between "ctrl" and "alt"
Love
High school

Escape: A Journey

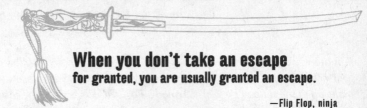

When you don't take an escape
for granted, you are usually granted an escape.

—Flip Flop, ninja

As entry is a penetration in, escape is a penetration out. Every out, in truth, is a new in. Many Homo sapiens "plan" their escapes the same way they plan their sex: in and out through Point A or in and out through Point B, if they have self-esteem issues. This is quite foolish and positively not the way of the ninja. Surprise is the corner-stone of escape. Surprise can also be enjoyable during sex, but for safety reasons is not part of its foundation. Therefore, when escaping, a ninja not only considers options A, B, and C, but also options Burbletwit and Wignafab. Confused by those last two nonsensical words? So will your enemy when you use them to escape. Ninjas train to see pos-sibilities where none exist.

Consider the following concepts as fluid guides for escape.

INFINITY

The only reason to escape is to get out of some-thing. The obstacles most enemies build to contain you are based in reality; a ninja escapes by accept-ing infinite and ridiculous possibilities *beyond* the realm of reality. We're not talking about a blind man in a hospital bed who imagines he has a win-dow through which he can see the world. We're talking about willing new truths into being that defy your enemy's expectations. If your pursuer believes a wall impenetrable, go through it. When facing great numbers that no man could defeat, defeat them. If the fall will most certainly kill you, don't die. Train for the impossible and impossible possibilities will happen.

For there was once a young ninja who was captured by a tribe of corrupt boarlocks* in need of some ninja bones they could use to cast a spell that would make all of the soup in the world explode. Foolishly, as is often the case, the head boarlock, Snort, decided to torture the youthful assassin. He sat the ninja on a

The ninja watches Brian (James Caan) in a wheelchair telling his wife, Joy, that he's gonna "beat this thing."

* Wild gluttonous warlocks found primarily in Arkansas who constantly feed their most base desires.

comfortable couch and made him watch the original 1971 made-for-TV film Brian's Song. *Snort's plan was to emotionally destroy the ninja and then debone him while he was still alive. The ninja, however, was trained in the Infinity escape philosophy. Once all of the boarlocks were seated and had their snacks, the ninja began to believe the possibility that watching two grown men share their feelings while one of them dies of cancer is NOT the most beautifully sad thing in the world for a dude. Using a technique called "rearing," he imagined that every line was being farted by a baby-butt-shaped mouth attached to each character. This allowed him to remain completely emotionally stable, even when Gale Sayers gives his Courageous Player of the Year award to Brian, knowing that he has less than a month to live. The boarlocks, on the other hand, were bawling, whiny messes. Their plan had backfired on them. Backfired to death, as a matter of fact. The young ninja quickly raced around snapping off all their tusks and jabbing them in their tearing, snotty faces.*

FRONT TEARS

Some men are really women. Some women are really demons. Some demons are tremendously misunderstood doors. A ninja knows that looks can be deceiving. Such is the idea behind this technique.* The name, Front Tears, is derived from the famous ninja Helen Gahn, who was unknown for her ability to feign crying so well that even a ladon† would become compassionate. She would then get herself close enough to her enemy to rip his face off. Escape becomes a lot easier when your opponent does not have a face.

The simplest application of this technique is to convince your opponents that you're trying to escape, when in fact you're trying to kill them, basically tricking them into pursuing you to their death. Now, you have to really sell that you're trying to escape, but you can't actually escape. It's a fine line. Especially if your enemy knows you're a ninja. You can't trip and fall because that's not something a real ninja does. This type of escape

---

* Not to be used for cheating on long-term committed partners.
† A seriously jerk-faced, unflappable dragon.

takes real acting. No horror movie naïveté and screams. Do not pull in a bunch of partners and pull a sting or an elaborate confidence scheme with fake betrayals and squibs. The David Crammit book *True and Near True* contains the following advice for a ninja trying to use the Front Tears method: *"Invent nothing and deny nothing, let your enemies' minds do the work. Your only job is to be the ninja your enemy thinks they can beat. In truth this will allow you to beat your enemy . . . often with their own limbs."* (Additional suggested reading: James Fliptem's *Inside the Ninjactor's Studio*.)

DEEP HEART SURE

It's extremely important to know when a mission is over. Think of each mission as a party. A party that you weren't really invited to but just heard about from someone else, and the dude who's throwing it doesn't know what you look like or that you have already killed his brother. A fairly specific way of thinking? You bet. Never be general.

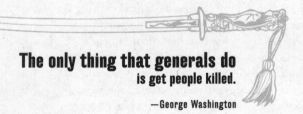

**The only thing that generals do
is get people killed.**

—George Washington

Specificity, and more specifically a specific feeling, is what this discipline is all about.

Deep Heart Sure is the art of getting the heck out of there. Rather than a technique, this is a honable feeling that heightens your ability to know when to leave. You are born with a seed of Deep Heart Sure in, as you might guess, your heart, but you must strive to develop it. Deep Heart Sure also slowly deteriorates as you get older. This explains why old people don't know when it's time to go (socially or permanently). Your DHS is directly linked to all of your individual emotions. These emotions, like school assemblies or moms, could save your life if you listen to them.

You must exercise and fortify your DHS to keep it strong and perceptive. If you don't, it will dissolve, and you will become a politician or a comedy writer. Or, if you use it incorrectly, it will warp, and you will call your ex-girlfriend way too much and name your car.

Listening to your Deep Heart Sure means that when you feel like you should jump, jump. When it seems time to run, run. When you sense that you're the only thing in the room that *doesn't* want to eat you, grab your covered dish and thank the host while using him as a human shield. Leave hesitation for Little League outfielders and the Clash. Nothing irks an enemy more than knowing you got away, except maybe you killing him.

Stealth

It's no coincidence that the first part of the word *stealth* is steal. A ninja thinks of stealth as stealing awareness from his mark. This approach requires a full understanding of what the mark could possibly perceive. Such understanding is especially important in today's modern world, where so many creatures are using tools to enhance their senses (i.e., infrared imaging, Seeker Nymphs, Laser Smelling).

Many dumb people ask, "If the ninja is so powerful, why does he need to hide, evade, or move secretly?" The answer quite simply is that stealth is one main reason the ninja is perceived as so compellingly able. We fear what we do not know, especially when we've also seen proof that it can kick ass. Ask yourself honestly which quote you find more disturbing: "I'm gonna tear your arms off!" or "   "?

Many people think "hiding" is the same as "not being seen." Wrong. Not being seen is easy. You simply don't go out and never do anything. You sit alone in a dingy apartment, eating beef jerky, managing your bit torrent files and playing World of Warcraft. Such is not the case with hiding.

Hiding is the ancient art of making someone or something hard to find. It is an active endeavor that takes extreme focus, heightened use of all senses, and years of creeping and slinking to master. Every creature hides something every day. A squirrel hides a nut, a vampire hides from sunlight, Steve Zhou of 2S224 Ludlow Street, Apt. 330, Cincinnati, OH 45202 hides his burning, obsessive, passionate love for Tina Williams, his blond-haired, green-eyed coworker at Smokestack Financial. But, as with all things, ninjas pursue hiding at its most intense level. They devote themselves to the art and science of Sneakiness.

The elements of Sneakiness are often called the three S's.

1. SURPRISE. Them not knowing is half the battle.

2. SECURITY. Strength from knowing things they don't know.

3. SPATIENCE. Space and patience. The most difficult to master, for it involves waiting and the room that is necessary for that waiting.

Whenever you're going to hide yourself or something else, consider these three elements. For centuries, sea pirates would "hide" their looted treasures on small, uninhabited islands. Ninjas would very quickly find the treasure and return it to the rightful owners. Why was it so easy for the ninjas to do this? Because the pirates ignored the second rule of sneakiness by placing giant *X*s to mark the spot where their booty be.

When a ninja is setting out to hide, he or she should hide in the exact same place every time: where they'd least expect. For example, people might expect you to hide near them, but not *ridiculously* near them. Here are some options for hiding around people.

ABOVE

BELOW

BESIDE

BEHIND

IN FRONT

There are 35 ninjas hidden in this picture. Identify each ninja and rank his hiding place in order of practicality for killing the horrid demon.

Whenever hiding, a ninja always wants to be comfortable and able to use as many senses as possible. If you're going to be hiding somewhere for a long period of time, you need to plan ahead with snacks, travel games, and a clean, quiet way to dispose of waste.

LET'S GET SMALL

Try using some of the following body origami techniques to get yourself compact enough to get into those hard-to-hide-in places.

The Briefcase

Reach down and grab your feet so that your body lays flat against your legs. Now bend your knees and elbows while tucking your head. Exhale with each fold to make sure your body is as slim as possible.

The Thin Man

Roll the right half of your body into the center front. Roll the left side of your body into the center left. Make the roll as tight as you need to fit behind the cloaking object.

Just a Head

Fold each leg, starting at the foot, up flat against the butt. Fold each arm, starting at the hands, evenly and flatly across the shoulders. Fold the entire torso in a rolling fashion around the butt. Fold the butt in half and then in half again four more times. Tuck the arm/butt/leg/body ball into the back of your ninja mask.

Finally, but not to be taken lightly, there are a few general places that you just plain don't want to hide.

- The first place they'll look.

- Places that stink really bad.

- Very very far away.

Do not let your ability not to be detected become a trap for voyeurism. You are not Kevin Bacon in *Hollow Man* watching the chesty chick or Kevin Bacon in *Wild Things* watching the chesty chick or Kevin Bacon in *The Woodsman* watching a kid. All the world *is* a reality show, but you are a player, not a viewer.

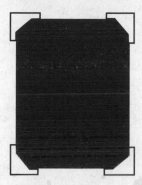

HIDEY'S DISEASE

I wish you could look at the face of this child, but you can't. You can't because this is Charlie and he has phase three Hidey's disease.

Each year, over five ninjas suffer from an uncontrollable, obsessive need to hide. It starts with a ninja believing he is so deadly that he must hide from himself and can progress to the point where the ninja is hiding from the very existence of his being.

Find out how you can help by allowing the Better Killing Through Education Fund to find you.

SECTION V

A butter scorpion looks for Texans.

10

The Worlds

There are many worlds, but just how many? That's a stupid question. That's like asking how many eyes you'll gouge out with your bare hands in your lifetime. It totally depends on the eyes, or, in this case, the worlds, you encounter. As Master Ukneevirse teaches, the quantity of anything is meaningless compared to how much of it there is. That may seem like a contradiction to the untrained eye, but a grain of sand could be worth 10 lifetimes of study with significantly vast meaning. Counting is a way of categorizing something without experiencing it; worlds are to be experienced and savored one by one. What good is it to know the number of ice-cream flavors if you have not tasted them? Everything is there for you to experience and you can never experience everything, but you should bust your butt trying until something stops you.

For there once was a virile young prince who was given every opportunity in his youth to see the world. But while preparing for each would-be journey, he would read everything about the destination and talk to anyone in his kingdom who had ever been there. If there were even one report of an illness, a bad meal, a poorly run hotel, or a person with thumbs, he would cancel his trip and begin to plan another. He never went anywhere. As he grew older, so did his fear of the world. Although he became a king of vast and beautiful lands, by the time he was 24, he was living in a 1 meter by 1 meter glass box that was constantly being washed by three naked, thumbless servants who were constantly being washed by three thumbless servants draped in bleached sheets with eyeholes cut in them. He had a thumbless food taster who would eat his full meals for him. If the taster did not die in three days, he would eat the food taster. Eventually, he had his thumbless servants cover his glass case with tar so that he would not worry about the things he saw in the room. Finally, he had the case dipped in molten steel and buried 40 meters underground with him in it. His last muffled shouts as they lowered the isolation container into the ground were "Make sure you pack the dirt nice and hard and don't leave any markers or indications that a hole was ever here." The food tasters sighed in relief and went on a group vacation to Switzerland, where they all died from eating a tainted, oversized dessert called Death by Chocolate.

There are several lessons that can be learned from that story. The first is don't go on vacation with coworkers. The second is that desserts with ironically ominous names can sincerely kill you. Thirdish, there are a lot of crazy-ass people/things in the worlds, and many of them attain at least some type of relative power. Whether they have opposable digits or not, avoid these people as allies and constantly plot to take any real influence they hold from them. Fourthlike, and most relevant to this chapter, you're part of the worlds. There is no possible way to separate yourself from them. Do not fear them. To fear the worlds is to fear yourself.

Now, that does not mean the worlds are yours. Just because you have a knowledge base that would drive a German scientist mad and skills more profuse than the acting range of Meryl Streep, that does not give you license to let the dishes pile up or not to chip in for pizza night. If you don't take care of the worlds, it inevitably leads to a situation where we can't have nice things around. And if there are not nice things around, that means there *are* not-so-nice things around, and not-so-nice things have a tendency to slice open your back and make bedroom slippers out of you while you're still alive. Several years ago, there was a ninja sent to guard the small Realm of Huh, a thin strip of invisible space that holds all the words people don't hear while talking to someone. Nothing much happens in this realm and the ninja got bored. He decided to have a few friends over, and it soon turned into a party that even Nero would say was out of control. Naturally, some of the guests started to pick up the unheard words and throw them around. Obviously, bad things happen when you start throwing words around, and it wasn't long before one of the words shattered a very fragile ego and tore a huge hole in the Fabric of Forgottenness. Roughly 45,000 unheard words spilled out and landed smack dab in the middle of the United States. Bam! The Civil War . . . or, as ninjas call it, the War of Phil's Royal Screwup. Although we were able to get rid of slavery in the process, it still took us five years to clean up that mess.

A Message from the Wind

Translated by Master Leaf Blower
The wind is a great and ancient ally of the ninja, a most honorable force that has both taught and served thousands of generations. It is cardinal for every ninja to listen to the spirit of the wind and meditate on its nature.

Yo, my ninjas!

What is *up?* I am so sorry it's taken me like forever to drop a line. What can I say, man? I'm the wind, you know. I gots to keep on with the keep on. Damn, it's been a while. You know I see all ya'll all the time out there doing your thing (can't hide from me. Gotcha! Just kidding). Seriously, though I'm always like, "Hey there's Black . . . you know, whatever. I should give them ninjas a shout." But then there's some hurricane that needs movin' or some sand that needs whippin' or . . . Ah, hell, look at me, busy ain't no excuse. We all busy as a mofo, you know. It's all good. You know, I'd rather be blowing than no going. Damn, you remember 20,004 years ago? We were all like, "This planet is boring, when is things gonna start bumpin'?" Now, shit, I'm like calling fire and water askin' 'em to cover stuff for me. That flooding in Kenya last week was suppose to be a dust storm. And, hey, you know Chicago, I completely forgot about it for like two weeks. It was like the Stagnant City. Total brain fart on my part. OH MY GOODNESS! Speaking of farts, I almost blew over a mountain when I saw the vid of Grand Master Kudamono's at the Firer's Club Roast for Snorge the Viking. He did that "demonstration" of the Ninja Passing Wind Technique and just went up to that fool and spun his ass in his face like he was gonna fart on him. Shit. That Nordic dork jumped back so fast he fell in the fire pit and burned his hair off. Classic. What am I talking 'bout, you were there. I hate when people do that. My bad. But it was off the wall. You gotta let me use that sometime.

Hey, yo, Cold wanted me to check with you about Halloween. What's your haps? Are you still down for helping us simultaneously give everyone in China a shiver of fear? You know it would be dope, but we can't do it without you guys. Let me know. We're thinking about meeting up in the Himalayas for a preparty and maybe chillin' in the Arctic Circle afterward.

I don't know if you've tried to hit me up recently, but I changed up my call. I was getting just way too many summons from special-interest witches about like global warming and what not. Are they serious? That's like stealing a million dollars and then asking someone if you can borrow a million dollars. You wouldn't believe the balls on some of these Spitches. Anyway, my call is basically the same, but you have to jump *from* the world while silently shouting "Swayze!" Don't give that out.

Listen, on the realsies, you my boys and I know those pirates ain't your crew, but you need to be telling them fools to quit bad-mouthing us. I'm gonna be where I am. It ain't my fault they have to sail around their ass to get to their booty.

I'm getting ready to head down to SoCal for the Santa Anas, which should be a good time if Fire doesn't go all fucking Rambo on me like he did last year. Hit me up sometime. I'm always around. Let's do this thing with Cold. Tell everyone around the dojo that I said WHOOSH.

Don't Spit In,
The Wind

An Instant Message from the Wind

Translated by Master Easy Breezy Lemon Squeezy

IM WITH UNKNOWN NINJA

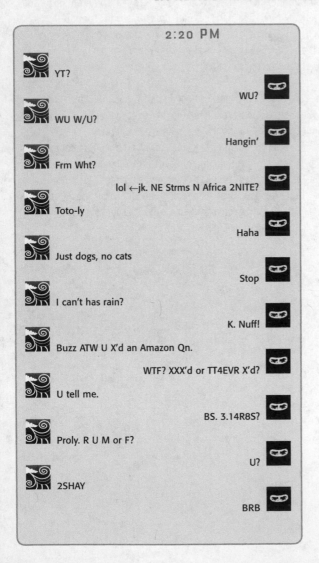

2:20 PM

YT?

WU?

WU W/U?

Hangin'

Frm Wht?

lol ←jk. NE Strms N Africa 2NITE?

Toto-ly

Haha

Just dogs, no cats

Stop

I can't has rain?

K. Nuff!

Buzz ATW U X'd an Amazon Qn.

WTF? XXX'd or TT4EVR X'd?

U tell me.

BS. 3.14R8S?

Proly. R U M or F?

U?

2SHAY

BRB

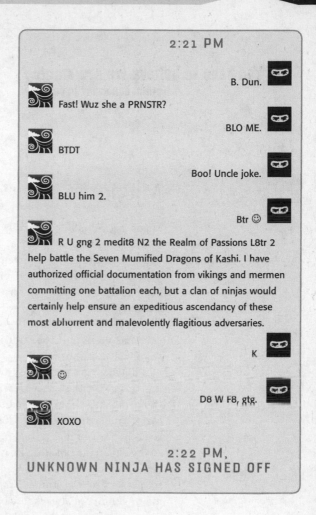

2:21 PM

B. Dun.

Fast! Wuz she a PRNSTR?

BLO ME.

BTDT

Boo! Uncle joke.

BLU him 2.

Btr ☺

R U gng 2 medit8 N2 the Realm of Passions L8tr 2 help battle the Seven Mumified Dragons of Kashi. I have authorized official documentation from vikings and mermen committing one battalion each, but a clan of ninjas would certainly help ensure an expeditious ascendancy of these most abhorrent and malevolently flagitious adversaries.

K

☺

D8 W F8, gtg.

XOXO

2:22 PM,
UNKNOWN NINJA HAS SIGNED OFF

A Video Postcard from the Wind

www.askaninja.com/wind

You have to believe we are magic /
Nothin' can stand in our way.

—Olivia Newton-John

Magic

Magic is a valuable tool that is all too often misunderstood by the outside world. To you, most likely, magic is a thumb that appears to come off of a hand or two macho gentlemen making white tigers disappear or a series of stories about a hesitant unspectacular fictional wizard. This is not magic. This is illusion.

Ninjas do not practice illusion. Ninjas practice the illusion of illusion. This is a difficult idea for non-ninjas to grasp, for they are so used to accepting things as they are presented, even if those things are not real (i.e., God or affordable health care). Similarly, if they are told something is not real, they accept it as unreal (i.e., Playboy Bunnies or the subterranean state known as Lower Texas). A ninja understands that there is always a reality present to everything. Embracing that reality allows a ninja to always focus on the moment and not presume what the next moment or the reality of the things in that next moment will be. Basically, we believe anything can happen. Not in a "Golly gee, my dog ate a rainbow and became the president of the Nation of Giggles" way, but in a "That chair might start a revolt and reverse the very idea of sitting" way. This opens up many possibilities for the moments and the things in those moments that have not taken place yet. That is to say, only that which is real can happen . . . but many only realize or are willing to accept a fraction of that reality.

If you see a ninja eat a cow before your very eyes, he has not tricked you into believing he has eaten that cow while actually putting the cow somewhere else. He has learned a real way to eat a whole cow. This is a very rarely used ninja technique, but it does have its practical applications. For example, the ninja master Phatee Bahtatee once disguised himself as schoolboy and swallowed a whole cow in front of a large crowd that his sarcastic enemy was hiding in. When the sarcastic enemy was compelled to make a snide comment, Phatee Bahtatee quickly threw some color blossoms on that ground that instantly bloomed and awed the crowd. As the crowd turned back to applaud the "boy," he had disappeared. The head of the man who had made the sarcastic comment fell to the ground with a loud thud, and the remainder of his body split in two and flopped in the dirt.

There are quite literally countless creatures that may be considered magic. It is important to realize that to them, they are quite unmagical and *you* may indeed be the magical one. Leprechauns, pegacorns, Hillary Scott. All of these beings perform amazing feats that many believe to be impossible. But they do them. Just because they may use an incantation or a spell or a glass rod with a 30-inch diameter doesn't mean they are not real.

Every ninja technique is based in reality. Whether *you* accept that reality or not is irrelevant if the ninja already has. Read the following story.

While casually walking through an Elven office birthday party for Allen Mossbottom on casual Friday, a wizard named Kato found himself surrounded by 12 cobra men that the elves had hired for security. Their necks were flared and their eyes glowing with unjustified anger. The wizard begged them to let him pass, for he had a hot date with Meg Ryan (circa Innerspace). The hissing hired hands refused. The wizard filled the tiny office space with water and conjured a gulp dragon, which proceeded to eat the cobra men. The fairies, who quickly had fashioned Allen's sheet cake into a boat, began to complain that they would soon drown and therefore miss the weekend. The compassionate wizard took a stapler and whispered in its ear. It immediately turned into a baby doll and drank up all the water and even slurped down the gulp dragon. She then exclaimed, "I have to whiz like a firehosey." And she ambled out the open window. The corporate fairies were not appeased and crucified the wizard with cubicle walling and caribou bones. The wizard smiled as they nailed him to the fabric-covered metal and whispered a reversal spell, which freed him and pegged all of the elves to crosses in a little circle. He then gathered the families of the elves and put them in a burlap sack with three starved shrews. As the fairies slowly asphyxiated on their tiny crosses, the last thing they heard were the screams of their loved ones being eaten alive. The wizard calmly walked into a coffee mug and gave Meg Ryan untold pleasure for three straight days.

Did you believe the story? You should. Although it never happened, it could have. There is, however remote, an outside chance that a wizard could've gotten a date with Meg Ryan at her hottest. That possibility is the very core of a ninja's edge. Never overestimate the limitations of truth.

Myth

The difference between a myth and a lie is quite simple. A lie is an untruth that must rely on its own strength for its endurance. A myth, however, is a mistruth that grows constantly in the minds and mouths of all who touch it. The world is full of such myths about the ninja: That our faces are so beautiful that we must wear masks to keep the world from exploding; that our urine comes out in vapor form; that we can turn both left and right at the same time; that it was a ninja who actually made *Raiders of the Lost Ark;* that ninjas sweat poisonous honey; that we fall the other way; that every time a bell rings a ninja is distracting you so that he can kill someone; that we can hide under wallpaper; that we've been there and done that; that we can IM with our minds; that the number *three* is a ninja; that we're actually a crack commando unit that was sent to prison by a military court for a crime we didn't commit and who promptly escaped from a maximum security stockade to the Los Angeles underground and are wanted by the government and who survive as soldiers of fortune and that if you have a problem, if no one else can help, and if you can find us, maybe you can hire us.

Some of those things are true, but *they are also all myths.* This whole book might be filled with lies, but the myth that it is not is what keeps you reading. You may even consider such a use of the word *myth* incorrect, but perhaps that is the biggest myth of all.

Now, seriously, if the ninja released all of our secrets to the world as blatant fact, creatures would begin to use them without proper study and universal balance . . . for evil, instead of for killing. A ninja seeks truth but lives in myth. Here is an actual ninja-to-ninja interview that shows the power of myth on your ability to get to the truth of a ninja master.

A STALK WITH GRAND MASTER POWER SWITCH

(contributed by the Ask A Ninja ninja)
One dark evening in the early autumn, I had the chance to sit on a very high tree branch and whisper with Grand Master Power Switch about the "myth" of the ninja. The following is our conversation.

ASK A NINJA NINJA: Psst. Grand Master Power Switch, it's me—
GRAND MASTER POWER SWITCH: Hiya!
    AANN: Unh! Ow!
    GMPS: Ya!
    AANN: Ahhhhhhhhhhhhhhhhh!

> *(Five minutes pass as I climb back up the majestic, 400-foot sequoia tree.)*

AANN: Hey, I told you I was coming to meet you here . . . at this time. Why did you attack me?

GMPS: Ya!

AANN: Ahhhhhhhhhhhhhhhhhh!

(Five minutes pass as I climb back up the 400-foot sequoia tree.)

AANN: Oh, I see. One must remain aware and ready even when the plan seems simple and safe.

GMPS: Who are you?

AANN: Wow. I guess I've never really thought about that. Let's see—

GMPS: You didn't see that eagle did you?

AANN: What eagle? Hmmm, I must have missed it.

GMPS: Poop on me in the middle of my dinner. I'll poop on you . . . [unintelligible but no doubt profound rambling follows].

AANN: I see. You know, it seems to me that being a ninja involves a constant conversation of body and mind.

GMPS: Shut up and don't move.

(We both sit in silence for what is best described as an awkwardly long time.)

AANN: You're right. I can really feel the connection in the stillness and silence.

GMPS: Crappers. It was just a stupid chicken hawk.

AANN: Interesting. I once read a scroll that described how you single-handedly destroyed two pirate ships full of murderous pirates using one chopstick, a piece of stale toast, and an autographed photo of Mae West.

GMPS: My grandfather would often run straight up a dinner roll.

AANN: Is that so?

GMPS: It certainly is. And there's a rock in the middle of the Horrortoad Jungle that can produce eyeglasses in about an hour.

AANN: Even as a ninja, it is hard for me to understand you. Your words would really not make sense to a non-ninja if they were to somehow come across our conversation.

GMPS: Yes, it does.

AANN: Uh, okay. You have never lived in a man-made structure. Why is that?

GMPS: The enemy who is against the laws of nature will lose the battle before he has a chance to fight.

AANN: Ah-hah. Now we're getting somewhere. I think I understand. That makes a lot of—Ahhhhhhhhhhhhhhhhh!

(Five minutes pass as I climb back up the tree.)

AANN: So, you might not have heard me, but I had said that I understand. Plus, I'm not your enemy, and this is a scheduled interview, not a battle.

GMPS: Shadow.

AANN: I'm sorry? Was that a response or a new line of thinking? Either way, can I get a bit more, you know, just for context?

GMPS: Anyway, I don't believe in novels or eras. (The great master makes a prolonged, loud, screeching eagle sound.)

AANN: Whoa. Um, is that because the constructs of man compare not to the truth of life?

GMPS: What was that chocolate, peanutty thing?

AANN: Uh, Reese's Peanut Butter Cup?

(Pause)

AANN: Ahhhhhhhhhhhhhhhhh!

(Five minutes pass as I climb.)

AANN: Payday? Ahhhhhhhhhhhhhhhhh!

(I climb up the damn tree again.)

AANN: Zagnut?

GMPS: Zagnut?

AANN: Yeah, Zagnut.

GMPS: Zagnut. (An odd little chuckle.) Zagnut. Zaaaagnuuuuut.

AANN: Yep. It's got—

GMPS: Zagnut, Zagnut, Zagnut, Zagnut, Zagnut. Beep beep. Zagnut. Zagnut, hooba baby, Zagnut. Zugnat.

AANN: Please enlighten me, Master, on what ninja meaning this candy bar holds.

GMPS: Who are you?

AANN: Hmmm?

GMPS: Ya!

AANN: Ahhhhhhhhhhhhhhhhh!

At that time, I decided to leave the great master to his brilliant meandering and find somewhere peaceful and on the ground to meditate on his powerful insights.

Ninja training and ninja life are full of "magical" experiences like that interview and magical experiences like throwing a dozen fleanixes* down the throat of an amazoff.† Experiences that seem so deep and mysterious that they grow into myths.

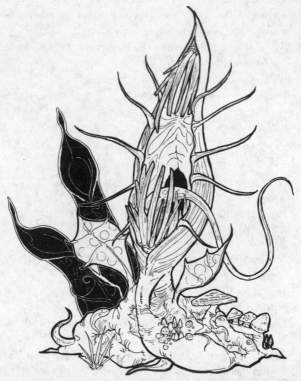

The "mythical" plantapus is an excellent ally to the ninja, who will occasionally have a very real need for the help of this giant carnivorous flower that dines solely on vegetarians.

---

* You cannot kill these little suckers.
† She looks like a normal Amazon, but is completely evil and criminally insane. Also sometimes called a "Hollywood Amazon."

Myths that become an extra shadow for the ninja to wrap himself in. A shadow born from truth that has no form from which to cast the shadow and no light to define its edges. And so is the ninja indefinable by anyone but the ninja. This is the power of Myth and Magic.

Myth vs. Fact: A Cinematic Look at Ninjas

With the exception of this book and www.askaninja .com, it is quite likely that everything you've ever heard, seen, or thought about ninjas is incorrect. If it is correct, it is by pure coincidence, but still impressive.

No medium has gone further in propagating falsehoods about ninjas than the silver screen (note: less than 4 percent of movie screens contain silver . . . and the lies continue!). The movie industry was built on tricks and overpriced concessions, things that the ninja, in essence, does not reject. The problem with ninjas portrayed in movies is the lack of, well, ninjas. You have heard the saying "The best lies are those wearing a T shirt that says truth." That basically sums up the issue ninjas have with their characterization in celluloid. We figured it would be best to address our issues in the manner that is most effective in reaching cinephiles—top 10 lists.

TOP 10 MISCONCEPTIONS ABOUT NINJAS PROMOTED IN MOVIES

1. NINJAS WEAR SCHNAZZY NONBLACK STUFF. No, they do not! Never. No red belts. No yellow sashes. No white guis for chicks. Black

and only black. Unless a ninja is in disguise as something else, like a president or a maintenance worker or a chick in a white gui. A real head ninja never distinguishes himself with a fancy robe with a golden dragon sewn on it; you can tell the head ninja by whoever is kicking your ass the hardest.

2. **HOMO SAPIENS CAN KILL NINJAS.** We're not saying it has never happened. It has. Exactly four times . . . all accidents. Definitely nowhere near the frequency or ease that is represented in film. And never by a sword!

3. **ALL NINJAS ARE JAPANESE.** That is offensive not only to ninjas, but to the entire Japanese population. The 3,000 islands of modern-day Japan play an important role in ninja history, but labeling ninjas as absolutely *anything* besides ninjas is the most extreme and disrespectful violation.

4. **NINJAS ARE "BAD GUYS."** Really? The Bill & Melinda Gates Foundation looks like a child slavery ring compared to the philanthropic efforts of the dark assassins. Ninjas are the givers and the takers of lives of takers. Put a ninja in charge and *Die Hard* is four minutes long and Mr. Nakatomi doesn't have to rebuild his plaza.

5. **ANYONE CAN HIRE A NINJA.** We're not the CIA. There is a process. There are forms to fill out and one heck of a review stage. Like Denny's, we reserve the right to refuse service to anyone. In actuality, the International Order of Ninjas rejects over 85 percent of the people that try to hire us. Of course, by reject, we mean kill. On a side note, unlike Denny's,

we will work with people who are not wearing shirts and shoes.

6. **NINJAS ARE CONSTANTLY AT WAR WITH EACH OTHER.** Are there ever mild disputes between clans? Yes. Are the resolutions always completely nonviolent? No. But for most intents and purposes, ninjas have no need to fight each other. They're ninjas. It's kind of like two glasses of water fighting over who's wettest.

7. **NINJAS FLIP AROUND FOR NO REASON.** You could build a city the size of Mexico with the amount of energy that actors portraying ninjas have expelled in movies. They do big running passes of unnecessary back hand-springs and cartwheels. They use aerials to do anything over one foot off the ground. Their favorite thing to do after getting hit is awkward flailing backflips. Can we flip? You bet your ass we can—front, back, side, in, and out—but a true ninja is economical with his resources and flips around only when it is the most effective maneuver or when impressing a ninja of the opposite sex.

8. **NINJAS FIGHT SLOW ENOUGH TO BE CAP-TURED BY FILM CAMERAS.** We could slow our movements down to 1/100th speed and it would be a distinguishable blur. The only thing more obnoxious than the inane slowness of cinematic ninja fights is the additional use of slow motion. For the love of lava, that's like writing a children's book about a dead mouse that doesn't go on an adventure. If you haven't already learned this about life, speed matters. Not only does the early bird get the worm, but also the late bird usually gets its wings ripped

off. Every single fight in the *Matrix* trilogy combined would be about 14 seconds at ninja speed.

9. **NINJAS PRETEND TO KILL PEOPLE.** In case you don't know, when a "ninja" kills a person in a movie, he's just pretending. That person isn't really dead. It's true. There is an actor by the name of Jason Cheng who has "died" at the hands of ninjas in over 45 films. When a real ninja kills, the thing being killed really dies. That's simple logic. Can you honestly say that Hollywood wouldn't be a better place if that were true? In 1999 alone, we could have freed ourselves of Hilary Swank's mannishness, Samuel L. Jackson's repetitiveness, Ben Affleck's oatmealishness, Bruce Willis's smirk, and Kevin Spacey's . . . well, just Kevin Spacey.

10. **NINJAS ARE NOT VERY VERY VIOLENT.** There seems to be this misconception among non-ninjas that honor somehow prevents ninjas from killing things in a horrific manner. We're talking about killing here, not casting a high school musical or even *High School Musical 3*. We often need to be and are quite brutal. The delusion has probably come to be because for the most part ninjas in movies are fighting people. We do. And we kill them. But, there are things a heck of a lot more dangerous than people that ninjas face. When we fight these creatures, we must slaughter them inhumanely (since they are in fact not human) and with no restraint. Ever meet a bean-nighe? Unless you're a ninja or dead, probably not. They're death fairies. They attach themselves to you as unremovable hats and summon death to your side. You can't just stab those puppies with a knife and deliver a witty

IS THE DARK KNIGHT ALRIGHT?

For decades, people have speculated whether or not Batman is a ninja. No, he is not. The Caped Crusader is a tremendously misguided rich guy with a really nice belt. His fighting uniform is ridiculous. The list of reasons he should be called the Dork Knight is endless, but here are a few key reasons why he is in no way a ninja.

- A flippity-flappity cape that is vain, cumbersome, and ... What exactly is it made of?
- His body armor screams lazy, and his headpiece greatly reduces range of motion. He turns like a whiplash victim in a neck brace.
- A ninja covers everything but his eyes, for his goal is to see life as it really is. B-dog covers everything but his mouth because he likes to yap. He will talk to anyone. Cops, kids, villains. If a ninja is there, he already knows why, and talk time is over.
- Instead of excelling in the art of Invisible Death, Batman uses the antiquated fighting form of Kung Pow, which causes large colorful bursts to fly from points of impact describing the sound each of those impacts make (i.e., Whammy! Boff! Spliff!).
- When is a ninja not a ninja? Never, because he's a ninja. But in case you are unaware, Batman is actually Bruce Wayne, president and CEO of Wayne Enterprises! He spends half his day pursuing the almighty dollar. A ninja can't be black and green.
- Very few fighting instruments are most effective when in the shape of a bat. Bat Rope doesn't even make sense. It's just a rope. There is nothing "bat" about it.
- Ninjas don't have aged butlers that pamper them and save their asses when the mission is too hard.
- Ninjas also don't have flamboyant, inept adolescent sidekicks. We have other ninjas. Somebody needs to let go of the old Bat Ego.
- If you need a huge light in the sky to tell you it's go time, you, sir, are no ninja.

I have spoken to a few actual batmen (they do exist). They are embarrassed and have asked the ninja to dispose of him on several occasions. The main problem is *The Badventures of Batman* is the most popular comedy program in I.O.N. It was created by a ninja named Penguinja, who videotapes all of Batman's missions and posts them on the Ninternet. It's like watching a sitcom, but it's funny.

one-liner like "Bean-nighe, done that." You have to destroy every shred of their existence by whatever means possible. You usually start by pummeling them with spin kicks until they are bleeding from every orifice. Then you turn them inside out and light them on fire. While they're burning, you shout insults at them while stabbing them repeatedly with an acid-doused sword. Next you pound them flat with a sledgehammer, pick apart each cell with an anthrax-infected needle, and feed it to a spiked-throat slug. To keep their spirits from coming back, you must then write a confessional journal of disgustingly perverse entries in their own hand and blood and distribute a copy to each of their family members. Is that very very violent? You bet your still-alive butt it is. Ninjas treat violence the way that Nick Lachey treats cologne: You can't ever use too much.

TOP 10 LEAST ACCURATE NINJA MOVIES

The opinions expressed below are those of one individual, the Ask A Ninja ninja. That being said, it is hard to imagine any dark assassin disagreeing with the following sentiments. Art is subjective, but gross negligence is unforgivable.

These are 10 movies for you to watch or rewatch in an attempt to better understand the atrocities perpetrated upon ninjas through cinema.

1. *AMERICAN NINJA* (1, 2, 3, 4, 5). It's not that Americans cannot become ninjas, but the ones that do never use nearly that much hair gel.

2. ANY MOVIE ASSOCIATED EVEN IN PART with Godfrey Ho or Joseph Lai (*Full Metal Ninja, Ninja Strike Force, Ninja Powerforce,* etc.). Yellow, red, and magenta guis! Where are

they hiding? In a bowl of Tropical Skittles?
The "ninjas" wear headbands, many of which
literally have the word *NINJA* written across
the forehead. Who is that for? If you're a
ninja, no one should ever see your forehead.
If they do see it, their immediate death should
be enough to let them know you're a ninja.

3. *NINE DEATHS OF THE NINJA* (1985). There
wasn't nine of anything in this movie except
bad times. From the modern dancers in the
opening sequence to the lollipop giveaway at
the end, nothing about this movie even whis-
pers "ninja." The most grievous ninja offense
is a battle with little ninjas where Shô Kosugi
is able to dispatch them in extremely short
order. Minjas are crazy deadly. You easily
need three or four regular-sized people for
each minja you plan on facing.

4. *YOU ONLY LIVE TWICE* (1967). The day that
anyone trained by the British government can
kill a ninja is the day I eat my own sword
sideways.

5. *MAFIA VS. NINJA* (1984). I chose this movie
to make a very specific point, since we are
almost always portrayed as the bad guys. The
"ninjas" in this flick run gambling rackets,
prostitution rings, and drug delivery services.
Real ninjas don't participate in any of those
activities. Think about it. We can transmedi-
tate through our selves to better understand
the essence of being. Do you really think we
have time to make illegal bingo cards and
pressure schoolyard punks into huffing gas?

6. *COSMIC SPACE NINJA 2: ESCAPE FROM
CHERNOBOURG* (1999). Too soon. In late
1998, an actual ninja named Captain Pain did

in fact save the universe from enslavement by an alien overlord with blue minions. Aside from blatantly stealing Mel Brooks's quotes, this movie is an affront to all who remember the events of December 5, 1998.

7. *TEENAGE MUTANT NINJA TURTLES* (all of 'em). It is completely unbelievable that they would wear silly Zorro masks instead of traditional guis.

8. *ROBOT NINJA* (1990). You can't replicate the real deal, baby, and both robots and ninjas feel that way about this movie. Only seeing two couch cushions sitting next to each other in an empty room can rival the excitement of the fight scenes.

9. *NINJA WARS* (1982). From blood spewing to vomit spewing, from decapitating to stabbing, everything in this movie is wrong. Devil Monks spit *balls* of vomit, not streams. I have seen head transplants, and this one was completely unrealistic (they used no robin leeches) and unnecessary. *Ninja Wars* was about as much of a war as watching two feathers fight over a butterfly using juggling scarves and about as pointless as well, considering that both of the main characters burn to death at the end.

10. *STAR WARS* (1977). How much cooler would the Jedi have been if they were ninjas instead of half-assed samurais? Much, I think. Plus, any ninja would have easily hit the thermal exhaust port on their first try. It was the size of a flippin' womp rat! Heck, I could've done it, without Han, if it were the size of Salicious Crumb.

TOP 10 THINGS NINJAS WANT IN MOVIES

1. Real flippin' ninjas.

2. More violence.

3. If someone dies, he actually dies.

4. No nonfight scene should be longer than 30 seconds.

5. No CGI. If you need to show a malice dragon in a volcano, get one and go there.

6. Everything shot in 4-D.

7. No plot holes.

8. No rehearsals before shooting.

9. Real weapons (bullets, swords, bombs, laser phasers, etc.)

10. Katherine Heigl (subject to change).

Things You Should *Not* Divulge About the Way of the Ninja

If you are a worthy entity, you should have no difficulty reading this.

Things You *May* Divulge About the Way of the Ninja

If you are a worthy entity, you should have no difficulty reading this.

The World and You

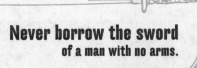

Never borrow the sword
of a man with no arms.

—Dr. Gripper, ninjologist

A ninja is never fit enough. A lifetime of physical fitness is a necessity for all shadow assassins. There are several merit badges for physical fitness in the *Black Badge of Courage Merit Book,* available only to the worthy who can endure the Ice Palace of Spring-Loaded Yard Sale Items and have $13.99 (exact change only). The following passage from the book addresses one of the most important elements of any ninja's exercise program.

Over three-quarters of the planet Earth is covered with water, and there is a whole mess of dangerous, mystical, and evil things in it. Therefore, to be a ninja, you must know how to handle yourself in the wettest places. Some of your most exciting ninja memories will be of water adventures, if you live to remember them.

I.O.N. WET AND WILD

1. **NO SUPERVISION.** Drown or be drowned. Every hand you need held is one you can't use for kicking aquatic asses.

2. **CONDITIONING.** Sure you can use spells and incantations to increase your speed and strength underwater, but if you rely on those things too much you're going to be screaming for your aunt Sally when a Chilean blob sucks all of the magic out of the ocean for 12 square miles. Nothing is more reliable to the ninja than good old-fashioned full-body conditioning. Remember, the thing you will be facing most likely lives, works, and plays in water.

3. **SWIMMING.** Every ninja must be able to exhibit squidlike agility and porpoise level speed to even be considered for any water mission.

I.O.N. BASIC SWIMMING TEST

Fully doused in tuna blood, drop into the middle of the Pacific Ocean. You should have 100-pound weights attached to each appendage and an additional 200 around your neck. Swim 20 kilometers on the surface with an average speed of 40 knots. Drop down 200 meters and swim 20 kilometers underwater without taking a breath and with an average speed of 60 knots. Drop down to the ocean floor and run 5 kilometers forward, 5 backward, and 5 shuffling sideways in each direction. Make sure you rapidly change direction by at least 45 degrees every 100 meters.

4. **AQUATIC FLOATING.** Levitation above water is not the same as levitation above land. You need to be allied with a friendly water spirit that is not of the physical world. Make sure she allows you the floatiness and freedom of movement needed to respond to anything zipping along the top of the water (pellicants), anything jumping out of the water (flying eels) or anything jumping into the water (electric sea lions).

5. **NOBODY SYSTEM.** Although many water missions require more than one ninja, you really want to ignore each other until it is time to attack. The reason for this is, it is tremendously hard to sneak in the water. Every time you move, you run the risk of moving the water around you. To reduce this risk, you must eliminate all extraneous motion.

6. **WEAPONRY.** Many of the weapons used underwater are modified versions of those used on land. Make sure to familiarize yourself with these weapons (by familiarize, we mean master). For example, water swords are actually made of sharpened water. They are excellent for stabbing shadow sharks, but they are also dang easy to lose track of in the water because they're made of the thing you are in.

7. **PLANNING.** Before a ninja gets even his isolated big toe wet, he should consider all water conditions pertinent to his mission. Below is an example of a properly filled-out Water Mission Planning Form. This is 1 of the 19 forms/requisitions needed to accompany a water mission.

INTERNATIONAL ORDER OF NINJAS
DEPARTMENT OF MISSIONS

Water Mission Planning Form   IMN: JK519®→4MS2

NINJA: *Red Rock*   CLAN: *Thunder Heart*

WATER

Fresh _____   Salt _✓_

Natural _____   Unnatural _____   Possessed _✓_   Enchanted _____

Black Water X X X X X ⊗ X X X X X X X X X X X X X Clear Water

Depth: 1,550 meters   Temperature: −40°C   Mood: School Girl

MISSION

Kill _✓_   Spy On _____   Retrieve _____

Person/Place/Thing *Mantataur Angler*

Proper Name *Eddie "the horn" Stinghoof*

Description: 6 tons, half manta ray/half bull, poisonous horns 40,000 lbs/sq. inch bite, 3 eyes (2 head, 1 tail), no sense of taste cave dweller, amorous, ears have teeth, magical ~~nose ring~~ nose ring ← (cloaking)

PLAN

I'm going to sneak into the Sea of Trankillity without a sound in the dark of night disguised as a sturgeon named Carl. I'm gonna swim up to him feigning a dorsal fin injury so that he eats me. Once inside, I'll slink into his second heart and shoot my bow of nine arrows (with bloodrope) into his first heart, both gill tendons spleen, kidney, belly button, brain stem, stomach and luminescent lure. Then I will jump out of his ear with the blood ropes and hook them to a speeding whiz whale (as of now, Bernie ~~Blubber~~ Blubber is in). I will hang on to the magical ring as Eddie's body is torn apart and ride it back to it's possessing source. I will then file a P44 scroll with the grand master who oversees that area or realm.

ADDITIONAL KNOWN THREATS

The Gulp Stream runs through the area and eats all lifeforms that cross its path. There are rumors of Eddie hiring several circular saw head sharks for protection.

Weapon Care and Training

Most modern weapons are made of materials that have not been double enchanted by the goddess Ovenia, a self-cleaning and self-sharpening spirit.* Therefore, blood and guts can accumulate all over your weapon. Additionally, even normal ninja use will dull the blade or wear out the wood.

CLEANING

You sure as heck do not want to do this in a place where you are likely to be attacked, but since that's everywhere, make sure you're loaded up with a bunch of other weapons before you start cleaning any individual weapon. If you're cleaning a sword, pack a handful of shurikens, a hanbo, a kama or two, maybe even a backup sword.

The best cleaning agent is most certainly Liquid Fear, which, as you should know by now, is found in the Great Chicken Lake. Just one drop can scare the spots off a leopard. Make sure you wear Valor Mittens† whenever using it.

SHARPENING

There is laser-sharp and then there is lazer-sharp. A ninja sword must be the latter. That Z, like those used by rappers, adds craziness, edginess, and danger. After all, what is Z but a pointy backward S. The only sharpening tool wicked enough to get you the Z you need is the testicle of a dragon. And if you think asking your parents for money once you're past the age of 30 is difficult, wait until

---

* Also possesses female poets.
† Made from only the bravest kittens.

you're running for your life with a slimy serpent nut stuffed in your gui and a severely pissed off magical reptile behind you. After you get your weapon lazer-sharp, make sure to dispose of the dragon ball immediately; if gotten wet or exposed to sunlight, it will immediately turn into a one-eyed purple-helmeted warrior snake whose sticky white venom can dissolve human flesh in seconds.

TRAINING

If you think you can just pick up a weapon and start cutting and whacking, you've got another thing coming . . . and it's probably in the form of that weapon as you end up cutting or whacking yourself with it, or when someone ends up taking it from you and cutting and whacking you with it. You need training, and for that you need a master.

Now, not every old man with a white beard who lives on a deserted mountain is a master, but it's a good place to start. Mountain masters are most often the best trainers in any ninja discipline. They are isolated, and because of that they have no one to bounce their crazy ideas off of. Therefore, they think that everything they imagine is profound and possible. That unjustified insanity is exactly the unmitigated gall you'll need to reach the ninja level.

For once there was a ninja who was stalking to his scroll club when he ran across a fat cutakiller, an insect named for the sharp backbone that many a ninja has cut his hand on when reaching for a branch. This particular cutakiller was binding itself up in a cocoon. The ninja felt sorry for the weird, icky bug and said, "Man, what a horrible life you have. I bet you wish you were a ninja." The ninja kept walking and did not see the hateful rage in the cutakiller's tiny little eyes. The next week, the ninja once again passed the same spot, but the cutakiller was gone. Suddenly, the sun was blocked, and the ninja spun around to find himself facing a humongous batterfly. "I don't need your self-aggrandizing pity," screeched the batterfly as it shot hundreds of baseball bats out of its abdomen at the ninja. The ninja rolled and quickly threw a perfectly placed plastic bag and suffocated the monstrous insect.

While training, never question your master. Questions slow the learning process and often lead to long tangential stories with flimsy relevance.

Here are what several crazy old mountain ninja masters had to say about training.

The only truth is pain.
That is why I answer every question by shoving a bamboo shard somewhere tender on the question asker.

—Ridicupain, crazy ninja master

Move the lake,
then eat the fish.

—The Whut, loony ninja master

One does not truly turn left
into an alley or jump down from a 12-story building or run up a wall. Direction is subjective.

—Possabilitree, nutso ninja master

Keep your urine close
and your enemies closer.

—Overstand, twisted ninja master

Kill one parakeet for every thing
you kill, excluding parakeets. When you have filled the well, you will be ready.

—The Flying Graveyard, mental ninja master

Death Aide

One of the toughest things for a ninja is watching another ninja die. It's boring, and there's most likely something more pressing that he should be doing with his time. That being said, it is equally aggravating for a ninja to die, especially slowly. After all, there's not much that ninjas like to do slowly.

Ninjas by nature are resilient and have many magical allies that can cure most common aliments, like a chopped-off arm or a dislocated personality. There are, however, times when a ninja *should* die. If you're around, you want to make sure that you do everything you can to (1) make your fellow ninja as dead as can be and (2) do it as fast as possible.

In order to facilitate your brethren's speedy demise, whenever going on a mission, you should prepare a personal Death Aide Kit.

The elements of the Death Aide Kit should be used in accordance with the following suggested techniques:

PERSONAL DEATH AIDE KIT

• Dagger of Death
• Bottle of water

AFFLICTION	REMEDY
Dragon eggs in brain	Stab head with Dagger of Death.
Serious burns (at least sixth degree over 100% of the body)	Stab heart with Dagger of Death.
Bite of a suspected zombie werepire	Stab head and heart with Dagger of Death.
Puncture wounds from blue cult oyster beak	Remove all joints with Dagger of Death.
Extra super extreme mega unimaginable shock	Tip over with Dagger of Death.
Returning *completely* inside out from the Realm of Annoyance	Poke repeatedly with Dagger of Death until ninja kills self.
Multiplane exponential dematerialization	Slice open each atom with Dagger of Death.
110% blood loss	Carve into eight even pieces with Dagger of Death. Serve with peaches and whipped crickets to Gloriole, the Princess of Pleasure.
Apathy	Dagger of Death. It doesn't matter where you put it or how.
Possession by Hurto, the demon of pain	Drown with bottle of water.

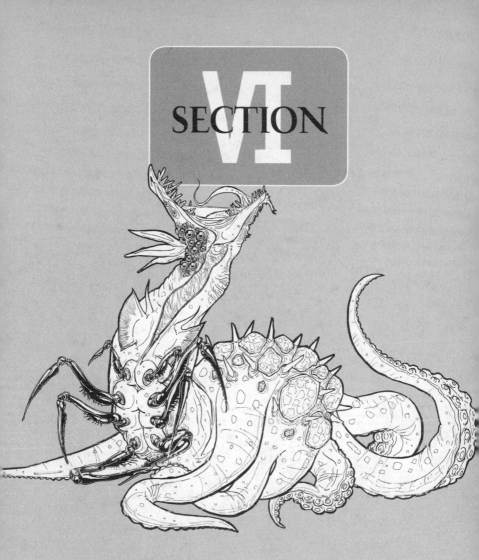

SECTION VI

A fubaripede warms up her voice for Killaoke.

Ninjaship

Sure, you're becoming like a ninja, but being a ninja isn't just about you and your clan going out and committing vicious yet utterly silent acts of murder and assassination. Being a ninja, like being a Scientologist or an Olympic curler, is an exciting opportunity to immerse yourself in a community far greater than yourself.

Welcome to the International Order of Ninjas!

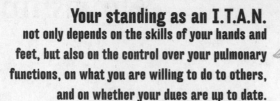

Your standing as an I.T.A.N.
not only depends on the skills of your hands and
feet, but also on the control over your pulmonary
functions, on what you are willing to do to others,
and on whether your dues are up to date.

—Double Trouble, twinja

Is I.O.N. in Your Future?

Are all ninjas just razor-sharp gingerbread cookies
with poisonous frosting rolling off a conveyor belt?
No! Part of the benefit of having an extremely
organized operation is strength through diversity. A single ninja doesn't have to do it all on his
own. This is not the International Order of Steven
Seagal.* The structure of I.O.N. is based on the
Concealed Open Platform (C.O.P.). It offers all the
benefits of a corporate structure without infring-
ing on your tweaked out individuality. Many hands
can hold more weapons. Do you like killing things
with swords? Did you have a blast the last time
you strangled something with your bare hands?
When you shoot an arrow, is it always a kill shot?
Maybe you're able to subtly drop poison into any
drink. Driving large objects through thick skulls
might be easy for you. Can you make people literally explode with your funny stories? Do your
friends respect your abilities in killing with bar-
bershop products? Perhaps you're allied with an
animal spirit and can transform into something
when you kill people. Every ninja is a wonderful
collection of talents, ideas, and experiences, and
C.O.P. can help you optimize both your productiv-

* A real organization. Membership: 1.

ity and your individuality. Let's say you're supposed to assassinate a hellamental* in Bangladesh
on Friday at 8:00 p.m., but you promised Suzy in
Phoenix, Arizona, that you'd take her out for a
strawberry phosphate at that exact time. I.O.N.,
like the individuals that make it up, is flexible.
It can facilitate coverage for either the kill or the
1950s-style date.

I.O.N. consists of seven completely unified areas
of awesomeness—each of which provides exciting
job opportunities for the ninja eager to make a con-
tribution to his community! Is one of them calling
your name?

DIVISION OF LIFE

All killing, exterminating, annihilation, oblitera-
tion, ruination, demising, and deathing starts and
ends with the Division of Life. This is where all
ninja mission plans are reviewed down to the last
dart. Division of Life staffers make sure every eye
is gouged and every tea is poisoned. They also follow up on every ninjassignment to make sure it
and everyone involved have been executed properly. If you're supposed to kill a baku† that has
switched to eating good dreams instead of bad
ones, and instead you off a bakru‡ who was just
weaving streams of light to run through, these
folks will find out and will make you write a tiny
but very heartfelt apology note.

DIVISION OF STUFF

This is the most coveted division in I.O.N. and is
often compared to the Feature Animation Group

---

* A living spirit made up of the seven elements of Hell (gluttony, greed, sloth, wrath, envy,
pride, and stupidity).
† A pink and black elephant-headed pig with huge pompadours that it is constantly combing
while whispering lines from *Grease* or *Grease 2*.
‡ The "Ghandis" of South American mini-spirits.

at Disney. This creative stronghold designs, tests, and approves all the cool-ass paraphernalia that ninjas use. They have designed and named over 75,000 different types of shurikens. And none of the names are trite numbering sequences. Each throwing blade has a cool and specific name like Sin Wheel, Whirligig, and Super Duper Spinning Star of Hell. They will construct custom devices to match any ninja need. A footless ninja had them develop two spinning saw blades that attached to his legs and rotated at 100,000 rpm when he flexed his calf muscles. Recently, they released a grappling hook made entirely out of assumption. As long as you reckon that the hook found something to latch on to and that it's sturdy enough to support your climb, it will. They are perhaps best known for their New Faces of Death demonstrations each year at Killacon.

DIVISION OF INVISIBILITY

If you can't see it, they are responsible. At least we think they are. No one has ever been able to confirm or deny the existence of this section of I.O.N. As a matter of fact, no one even knows how this passage got into this book. Or did it.

DIVISION OF EXISTENCE

Besides validating and verifying all known and reported life in the universe, this area of I.O.N. also manages all realms, planes, and dimensions with respect to their influence on reality. For instance, in 1823, the D.O.E. found a small, shivering ball of Teen Angst somewhere in the Realm of Y-Mei. Today, it is a thriving, productive member of the Alliance of Emotions and recently wrote an epic poem entitled *Uneasy Rider*.

KILLER COMMUNICATIONS

The business of black is to be unknown, but in order for that to happen the unknown must know itself. For if the right leg does not know what the left ear is doing, one of them is going to get cut off. This department handles everything from intelligence gathering to communications and information dispersal. It is not an easy task keeping silent, invisible people in contact.

COUNCIL OF SHADOWS

These are the big boys. The Council of Shadows is made up of all of the grand masters. Dead and alive. It is said that the entire council is in constant communication through a meditative conference call. All ninja missions must be approved by the council. They assess threats, oversee training, and maintain the peace and honor that ninjas cherish so deeply. The entire council only meets in the same physical location once every one hundred years during a ceremony called the Wet and Wild Weekend Bash.

THE BLACK BOARD

The Black Board is an elite team of unknown numbers. The ninjas in this unit have one singular mission: to keep ninjas on their toes. They have complete access to *all* areas of I.O.N. They have license to test any ninja at any time by any means: Your candy drawer is suddenly full of vipers. All of the weapons on your person become enchanted and begin attacking you. Kicking you in the butt while you're peeing. The second you think you know everything, you become nothing.

I.O.N. Top Brass

Although there are over 300 grand masters in the Council of Shadows, there are only 5 that oversee the day-to-day operations of ninjas at a corporate level. If you want to become part of I.O.N., get to know them and then stay out of their way.

GRAND MASTER KUDAMONO (NICKNAME: CARMEN MIRANDA)

The modern faceless face of ninja. G.M.K. earned his notoriety as a teenager during the Robot-Clown Struggle of 1893. He has terminated over 100,000 things justly and with wicked style. His favorite saying is *"We live in the darkness we create."*

GRAND MASTER GOLDEN PALM (NICKNAME: THE PROCEDURE)

Hands down the most prolific ninja writer/documentarian. He can write five separate thoughts simultaneously in five languages using his feet, hands, and nose. His famous Golden Palm Technique is a noncontact air punch that when mastered can tear flesh from bone from 100 meters away.

GRAND MASTER FLASH (NICKNAME: SUGAR BUNS)

Aside from being a renowned "ladies' ninja" Grand Master Sugar Buns's knowledge of blackness is tough to rival. He presides over the prestigious Nowhere Clan. He is the only ninja to ever travel at the speed of darkness.

GRAND MASTER METALIKILL (NICKNAME: SANDMAN)

"The most rock 'n' roll sensei in the business," says Pains Hatefield. Arguably, no one kills harder than this full-tilt ninja. As the founder of the Thrash Rock Clan, Metalikill has trained such famous ninjas as Meg of Death, Ann 3 Axe, and Slay Hurt. He is also an accomplished musician and recently put out his 45th album, *Light the Puppets,* available on dieTunes.

GRAND MASTER LYLE (NICKNAME: MR. BIG TIME)

Try to match wits with this ninja master and you will find yourself brain-dead before you can say, "Um." Feared for his Binary Fingers of Death, in which he actually reprograms your body to beat itself to death with strategic digit strikes, Big Time conceived and produced the popular Web series *Aok A Ninja.* His gaming skills have been called "Krueger-esque" for their ability to kill a character so hard online that he dies in real life.

Be Careful What Door You Try to Get Your Foot In

You should be warned: Every door at I.O.N. has a king clown snake behind it. A real one. It is a safety precaution that has served the Order well since the days of Ninjankhamun. Bites from the ubiquitous vipers are extremely likely. Each one usually tries to devour at least one human a day. They strike when they sense loneliness. There are 10 different varieties of king clown snakes that slither-guard the passageways of our dark halls. Here is a short rhyme to help you quickly and easily recognize which type of king clown snake you are facing.

Red and Black will quickly attack
Red and Yellow will slowly eat a fellow
Red and Blue will asphyxiate you
Green and Red will bite your head
Yellow, Blue, and Green will burrow into your spleen
Orange, Black, and White will deliver 500 cc's of nerve
toxin with its first bite
Sea Foam, Magenta, and Reddish Brown will spit
down your throat until you drown
Amaranth, Olive Drab, Viridian, and Kale will whip
you mercilessly with its tail
Olive Drab, Amaranth, Viridian, and Aquamarine
will drive you insane as soon as it's seen
Viridian, Aquamarine, Amaranth, and Olive Drab
will give you endless wealth if you grab

Ninternship Graduates

One of the best ways for an I.T.A.N. to get a job with I.O.N. is to complete the legendary I.O.N. ninternship program. It is an intense experience that if completed will leave you prepared for anything this life and most others throw at you. The program has no set time frame—or any other parameters, for that matter. Once you apply, you're not told whether or not you've been accepted. If you are accepted, you're not told when the ninternship begins, what it entails, or when it is over. The one promise that I.O.N. makes to its ninterns is guaranteed hands on throat ninja interaction.

There have only been three people to ever actually finish the ninternship program: Joan of Arc, Benjamin Franklin, and Danny Grant.

When I left the ninternship program, my master told me, "Joan, the best portions of a good ninja's life are small, unremembered acts of death." But still I tried to change the non-ninja world with massive carnage and brilliant killing. It didn't work. Sure, I became famous, but what really changed? I still remember thinking, as I escaped from burning at the stake with the Invisible Flame Jump, "They will never learn until they stop spending all of life preparing for death." Since then I have devoted myself to following my master's words, and my undocumented missions and kills since that moment on have brought me happiness and fulfillment. I will live the rest of my days as ninja as possible and mostly in Australia.

—Joan of Arc (1/6/1412—unkwn)

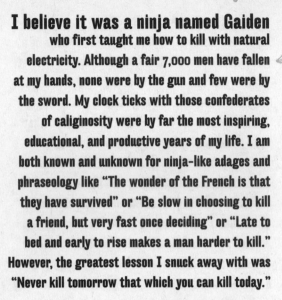

I believe it was a ninja named Gaiden
who first taught me how to kill with natural
electricity. Although a fair 7,000 men have fallen
at my hands, none were by the gun and few were by
the sword. My clock ticks with those confederates
of caliginosity were by far the most inspiring,
educational, and productive years of my life. I am
both known and unknown for ninja-like adages and
phraseology like "The wonder of the French is that
they have survived" or "Be slow in choosing to kill
a friend, but very fast once deciding" or "Late to
bed and early to rise makes a man harder to kill."
However, the greatest lesson I snuck away with was
"Never kill tomorrow that which you can kill today."

—Benjamin Franklin (1/17/1706–unkwn)

Fear not, I am watching.
Fear, I am watching.

—Danny Grant (8/28/92–present)

Personal Development

SURVIVAL

In the late 1300s, an ancient scroll over 1 million years old was found by a ninja in a cliffside cave that is now a McDonald's/Starbucks. Ninja scholars labored over the list, deciphered it, and revealed a list of things essential for survival. This is the list.

1. Stay alive.

The simplicity and profound truth of that list has guided ninjas for centuries. You may have all the skills in the world, but if you are dead they're hardly going to do you very much good at all. You must not only memorize this list, but you also must live by it. If you need further encouragement, know this. The ancient scroll was found with the bones of the *dead* author. The very writer of the words was not able to abide by them. Can you?

SUPREMACY

To the ninja, excellence is a necessity, not an option. Being the best isn't about knowing you're the best; it's about *being* the best. That's why the ninja motto is BE. Supremacy involves three things: Control, Awareness, and Extremeness. **Control** can come in many forms and should never be confused with power. It is the power behind the power. **Awareness** is the foundation of supremacy. There is a ninja proverb that says, "If you can't see the bottom of the mountain, how do you know you are on top?" **Extremeness** is the unrelenting pursuit of the awesome and ultimate. By the time you are an I.T.A.N., you should be able to put "extremely" in front of every skill you know.

The spirit of ninja supremacy is eloquently expressed in the following phat rhyme.

MC U-NO-C, PIONEER NINJA RAPPER

SONG: KILLER JAM

ALBUM: STRAIGHT OUT OF NOWHERE

Here I go
Here I go
Here I go
Here I go

Check the noize from the boyz with the toys dat kill
If ya wantin' mad blood you gots to pay the bill
My skills get ill fillin buckets with brains n guts
My right foot be gettin tired from kicking butts
Switch left, just as def to bring about death
What's that you're saying with your very last breath
Oh snap, there goes your neck and your knee
I'm the last thing you saw and you didn't even see
Me really cause I'm fast like a racing car
I'm near then far, then BAM! Throwing star
In the forehead, dead is what they just declared you
So quick, didn't even have time to scare you
Where you running there is no escape
Like a momma lion I pick ya up by the nape.
But whoops I accidentally grabbed your spine
Prognosis is Oh, shit, you're really not fine
You're dying for realies but also for my lyrics
You wish your life was longer just so you could hear this

Killer Jam *(repeat 13 times, not including the ethereal homegirl echo)*

Droppin' back in like a kracken wakin from a deep nap
Slap slap I'm all over you like Google maps
Surveillin' tailing I know all ya moves
I know that its rough but I'm so damn smoove
Like the butt of a baby ain't no maybe with me
Think I'm a tree slice slice you got blood in your pee
Slow down, let me think, I don't think so
Slow-mo is a no-go for the way that I flow flow
I'm talking rapid ripping quickly and kicking
Get out the way to avoid blood dripping
On my fresh threads I got a whole damn file
Of suckers I made dead just from checking my style
Spinning forget about it I'm a tornado times five
No one's rebuilding cause there's no one alive
Pulling in honies like I pull off arms and legs
Yank you, thank you, I know a guy who sells pegs
Got your nose, got your ears, got your heart
The only thing I left you with is a fart, let's go

Killer Jam *(repeat 13 times, not including the ethereal homegirl echo and the robotic synth voice)*

This jam is called killer there's a pretty good chance
I'll kill you, but first you must do the Killer Dance
Pull out your naginata and wave it in the air
Really fast in a circle like there's somebody there
Throw a smoke bomb run around behind ya honey
Punch her in the nose and take all of her money
Do the windmill at 60 knots
With spikes on ya heel now check what ya caught
(repeat)
Signing autographs before they even ask
A ninja spinning hits so fast he be melting the wax
Twenty-four sev I be chasing the dream
Death without a breath or the thought of a scream
Linguistic assassin but also one for real
Got rhymes that kill backed up by steal
You no see me U-No-C see you
I stop hearts on the charts just doing what I do
You can live like a ninja or die like a bitch
This jam is the decipherer to figure out which

Killer Jam *(repeat 13 times, not including the ethereal homegirl echo, the robotic synth voice, a group of British schoolchildren spelling out the words* killer *and* jam *and rowdy yes-yes-ya'lling by guest rapper Tupunch Shuirk'N)*

Killer Jam *(repeat 13 times while it sounds like the song is slowly being dissolved in a vat of acid)*

CHANGING LIVES

Many ninjas won't tell you that changing lives is really what ninjaing is all about. Whether it's changing something from alive to dead or legged to legless, every ninja's goal should be to have everyone they encounter walk, scoot, or be carried away a changed person. This is a commitment that helps maintain excellence amongst the dark assassins.

Lots of people have had an arm chopped off, but how many of them had it chopped off by a ninja? If they did, we want it to have been a special experience that really impacted their life.

This is why a ninja master must review your mission form before you even start polishing your grappling hook. Ninja masters ask the tough questions that keep all ninjas honorable, righteous, and cool. Questions like: Does this person need to be killed or merely extremely wounded? What if this encantado* has a brother? Left hip or right hip?

Aside from listening to your masters, there are always things that a wannabe ninja of any level can do to change lives. Most people are too stupid to realize that no one is going to change their lives for them, so it's up to ninjas to step in and take care of the job.

Push People
Sure, actually, physically pushing someone can greatly change his life, especially if there's a stairway nearby with tetsu-bishi† at the bottom, but what we're talking about here is psychology. Asking personal questions to delve into the "uncomfortable" areas of people's lives. Prodding until you not only find their "buttons," but also discern the most agonizing way to push them. A ninja looks for patterns and exploits them to drive people insane. Hygiene patterns. What if every time a specific vegetarian went to the bathroom you slipped an apple in the toilet in between their doing their business and flushing? That will really mess with someone after a while. (It's a commonly known fact among ninjas that all vegetarians look before they flush.) Sleeping patterns. How about whispering the word *Montana* in someone's ear while they sleep for five hours every night for five

---

* Spirit who comes from the paradisiacal underwater realm called Florida.
† Small spiked weapons shaped so that one sharp point is always facing up.

years? You can bet your bokken that the next time you need to find them, they'll be running naked through the fields of the Treasure State. Internet browsing patterns. Do you have any idea how crazy someone goes when no matter what computer he's on, every search takes them to a picture of Kermit the Frog eating a ham sandwich?

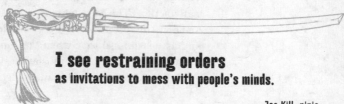

I see restraining orders
as invitations to mess with people's minds.

—Joe Kill, ninja

Prepare Them

Surprise is a great tool of the ninja and one that should never be undermined, but there is also a Zen-like beauty in stealthily aiding a beast in preparing for an inevitable change. Creatures fear change, and if it's gonna be a change brought about by a ninja, they have good cause. Play into that fear by changing the world around them. Erase their iPod, send horribly offensive e-mails from them to everyone they know, burn down their house. These are the subtle clues that can help a person prepare for a much-greater change. Also, killing someone close to someone you are going to kill can often get them thinking about death, in a good way.

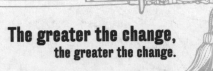

The greater the change,
the greater the change.

—Die Chart, ninja

Show Them a Good Time

Often, you're one of maybe two ninjas in the world that know about a tremendous change coming someone's way. Isn't it up to you to make sure that the change is indeed as tremendous as possible? If someone slaps your head, that is not nearly as impactful as if they do it while handing you an ice-cream cone. Send your mark large sums of money, find them love . . . or at least sex, give them job satisfaction. The idea here is to make your soon-to-be victim feel as positive and fabulous about his life as possible so that when you rain your ninja wrath upon him, it is truly soul destroying. That is true hard-core change, ninja style.

SECTION VII

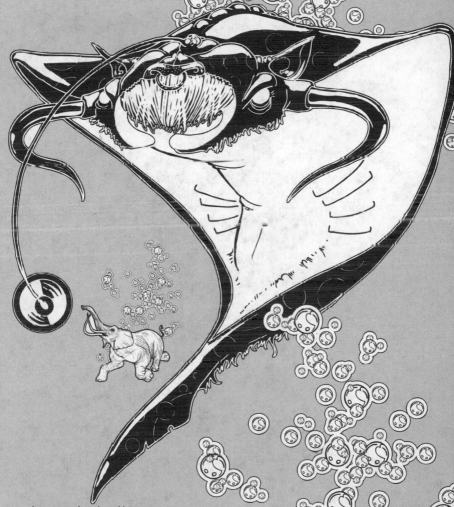

A mantataur closes in on his prey.

12

The Mission*

And so here you stand
A containerless, cogless fluid kind of thing
A form upon which masters have operated
Leaving the few parts that worked
Replacing all others with better, stronger, faster parts
Now set loose upon the darkest corners
With a mission†

The function and greater mission of all ninjas is to sustain and improve all life. This is accomplished by going on many smaller missions full of killing and kicking ass.

You are now on an endless mission whose only payment will be satisfaction and stories. It is a lives-long journey that will gradually teach you everything you can know about everything.

---

* Impossible.
† This book will self-destruct when you least expect it.

That's a good thing. If the collective knowledge of the ninja were thrust upon you in an instant, you would implode into an infinitely diminishing string of insanity. Embrace the idea of the mission the way a swooping eagle embraces a plump baby. For the mission, like that baby for the eagle, will feed you and keep you coming back for more.

Only through your smaller missions will you ever really experience the bigger mission. The smaller missions you go on will be divided into three main categories.

- **Ninspionage.** Ninformation gathering. Surreptitiously or boldly acquiring intelligence about the enemy. Every foe is worthy of some discovery, from a leviaphant* to a woman.[†] Ninjas like to think that they can learn something from everyone before they kill them or ferociously pummel them about the head, torso, and limbs. Mark Twain once said, "A little knowledge is a dangerous thing." It's even more dangerous when it's in the hands of a ninja.

For once there was a caninja[‡] named Fast Deadie who was hell bent on beating a flininja[§] named Spinnesota Splats in a game called Killiards.** He played him dozens of times but always lost because he knew nothing about that old Splat Cat. Finally, he took the time to find out that the indomitable pussy was left-pawed. Before their next match, the caninja bit off the left legs of the masterful Midwestern mouser. Now, although Spinnesota bled to death before they could actually play, the deadly dog knew that he could have probably beaten him.

- **Ninjabotage.** Disruption of others' plans or processes. If you can cause a fight between Mr. and Mrs. Dragon on Tuesday, chances are that they'll still be at least thinking about it when you battle them on Wednesday. Blowing up a

---

* Large sea mammal who never forgets.

† Large land mammal who remembers every single goddamn thing you've ever done or said.

‡ A dog that has trained in the ninja arts (not man's best friend).

§ A cat that has trained in the ninja arts (no friend at all).

** A tremendously violent sport that involves whipping hard balls at the groins of 16 random people.

guard post of a jungle prison could be the difference between stabbing and getting stabbed. Infecting an evil genius's computer with an ACCATT program (All Chris Crocker All the Time) could save the lives of millions. These missions are about stealing the painting of what your adversaries want and replacing it with a photo of you punching them in the face.

- **Assassination.** Killing with honor and lots of cool moves and neat weapons. And, needless to say, the ability to get in and get out stealthily with cool moves and neat weapons. Assassination is called the "rock star" of the ninja techniques, but to a ninja it is a time- and spirit-honored practice. Taking a life is easy; taking the right life is a lot harder.* A good assassination is like a good wine: Its stains should be very very hard to get out. Let each kill be a symphony. A blindingly fast, painful symphony, played with instruments of death and conducted by an invisible maestro

* Taking the "right to life" is near impossible.

Time Line
of Ninjas

In order to know where you're going, you must make some attempt to understand where you have come from. History can often tell you why you have chosen this path and what painful lessons you are bound to repeat.

The following passages are excerpts from *From Nothing to Nothing: A Ninja History.*

Dawn of Death

No one knows the exact origins or dates of the first ninja. Many scholars believe that this stealthiness is exactly what makes them the first ninjas: If they had left buildings and pots and graves, they would hardly be considered ninjas. There are, however, five tablets of stone carved by a human hand that were discovered in a cave in the Galápagos Islands in 1406. The cave was very well booby-trapped, and as a matter of fact, the first 83 ninjas that attempted to enter it died. Their deaths are recounted in the essential coffee-table book *The 4,000 Most Important Deaths of 1406*.

The tablets were finally found a full mile underground in a completely sealed room that contained, aside from the tablets, a black gui made entirely of stone, a stone guitar, and a petrified lemon. The tablets, which became known as the Ninjetta Stones, are written in an ancient language that consists entirely of three-dimensional pictographs.

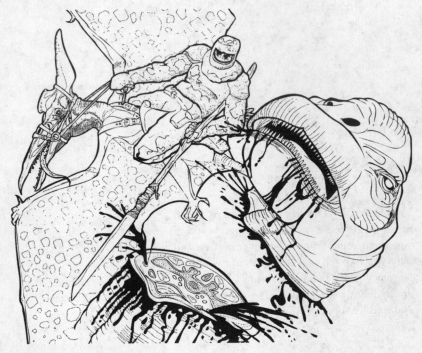

One hand-carved cell of the Ninjetta Stone.

The pictographs tell the tale of a clan of "people" who developed skills and thoughts that transcended those of any of the creatures they had encountered. No beast was a match for their weapons, and their lives had become a committed search for a worthy foe. No tale is told of where exactly they came from or where they went to. Although this is still actively debated and discussed, many believe the final carving on the last stone is that of an ancient smoke bomb going off—a sign or symbol that they purposefully disappeared with aims not to specifically be discovered.

These stones depict a lifestyle that is a far cry from that of the modern ninja. We can tell from the pictures that these ur-ninjas had a crude form of meditation that only contained four alternate realms: Earth, Wind, Fire, and Water. The weapons depicted are sharp and deadly, but almost entirely made of stone. They passed their knowledge down from generation to generation using complex verbal explanations. Although the modern ninja may laugh silently at the clumsy and savage ideas and techniques, one cannot review the findings without wondering if the "people" who left them were the killer ancestors of the silent, deadly assassins most know so little about today.

Homo Sapien/ Killersapien Divergence

Science has many ways of classifying the various life-forms in the known universe. There are kingdoms, phyla, species, and genera, just to name a few.

Very little of this matters to the ninja, especially as we trace our history.

The one point of interest in this arena to the ninja is the apparent separation of the dynamic from the stagnant members of life. By this, I mean those who have chosen to pursue every breath of life with the fierce intensity of a thousand shooting stars, and those who are willingly dazzled by the mediocrity of Jennifer Lopez.

There was a time, an era, and an epoch when those who were content with sameness—homos—separated from those who demanded awesomeness—killers. It is very important to note that while scientifically the term *killer* does mean causer of death, academically it simply refers to any life-form that constantly seeks more perfection out of life. Kind of weird, huh? A term that many today look upon as a negative way to talk about takers of lives is actually derived from a word meaning seeker of life.

The divergence was not an overnight process. It took about a week. In that week, the various Killersapiens took steps to separate their civilizations and lives from the dumb stuff the Homo sapiens were doing (or not doing). This divergence was a natural occurrence of evolution and was not organized. It happened because it needed to happen. Those who seek the ultimate will organically move away from those who make complacency their goal.

History, like a ninja,
will always surprise you and then kill you.
—Mark Twain

The divergence between the two groups of sapiens is important for many reasons, the greatest of which is that it is very hard to pursue astonishing brilliance when there are a bunch of idiots in your way. When the two species began to diverge, the Killersapiens had a choice: whether or not to completely dispatch of the Homo sapiens permanently. Some say it would have made everything a lot easier to simply kill all the Homos. Maybe, but that was not the way of the Killersapiens, at least not the ninja portion of the species. As a matter of fact, this moment in history marks the extending of a zealous olive branch of fiery fire to all Homo sapiens, inviting them into the fold of mind-blowing kickassitude, should they ever choose to stop watching sitcoms.

Below is a list of the major groups of Killersapiens. Please keep in mind that only a few examples are given for each classification. Also, many life-forms are members of more than one group.

MAJOR GROUPS OF KILLERSAPIENS	
WARRIOR	You say where, you say when, and they will be there with hell's bells on. Notable examples: Amazons, vikings, clowns, leprechauns, sharks, sequoia trees.
OMNISAPIEN	These are technically members of both the Killersapien path and the Homo sapien path. Notable examples: werewolves, rugby players, robots, venus cat traps, jellyfish, and Canadian comedians.
NINJA	If there were superlatives for Killersapiens, ninjas would win Best and probably Most Likely to Succeed. Notable examples: Every single flippin' one.
CORKY	God bless 'em. These are the goobers who try and try and never give up. No matter how bad they are at being awesome, these lunkheads just keep plugging away. Notable examples: pirates, trolls, ogres, supermodels, and zombies.

MAJOR GROUPS OF KILLERSAPIENS	
UNKNOWN BEAST	The scary stuff. Relentless and hard-core. Notable examples: dragons, leviathans, fairies, unicorns, and kudzu.
MIX	Any combination of two or more Killersapiens. Notable examples: merpeople, centaurs, elionphants, bearhawks, and cameleopards.

As far as classifying Homo sapiens, it's not really worth the effort. For whatever minor difference there may be between them, the overriding fact that they are so lame makes any exercise in discrimination futile.

Big Bam

There was a fight. No one knows exactly who started it, but it had something to do with a Chinese fox pissing off the very concept of Sleep. For those of you who are not aware, Sleep is not necessary. Sleep is actually a giant organism that lives off of dreams. Sleep arrived at Earth about 4 million years ago and forced every creature on Earth into a full-time REM state. After much debate and some pretty nasty nightmares, the Killersapiens were able to broker a deal by cornering Sleep in an underwater cavern.

The Killersapiens were able to negotiate Sleep down to one-third of every creature's life. Cats offered to pick up the slack for any life-form that was physically unable to sleep (e.g., the Giant Eye of Behind).

Anyway, they were about to sign the contract, but this shape-shifting vulpine did something to offend Sleep and subsequently Sleep left.

It was hurt.

It needed some time to work things out.

Well, suffice it to say after having Sleep for several millions of years, you begin to rely on it. So, without it, everyone got really cranky, really quickly. Little skirmishes were breaking out everywhere. Dwarves were punching banshees, winged snakes were eating cyclopes, sphinxes were asking people unsolvable and personal questions like "What has your ineptness at correspondence in the morning, your annoying self-centeredness in the afternoon, and your weird thoughts about your cousin in the evening?"

After about a week, all of the little rumbles had escalated into a worldwide battle royale. This was the first—and if you ask the majority of Killersapiens, the only true—world war.

It was on.

From the Continent to the Ocean and from tropical pole to tropical pole (the climate and topography of the world was a bit different back then), everyone was fighting.

It was like a two-year-long Thanksgiving dinner.

Sure, there were small lulls and calm moments, but then inevitably someone would bring up the time Cousin Mike got arrested for prostitution and BAM the fighting would start again.

That's where the era got its name. Every time you thought it was over, BAM a bodach* would crash through your wall wielding a folding chair. Many thought that this was it. The end of life. We would just fight ourselves right into extinction.

The one group that did not choose to accept that pessimistic fate was the ninjas. It was during this period of extreme unrest that ninjas really began to develop their sneakiness and hidiness. Not that ninjas were afraid to fight, but when everyone in the world is trying to kill you, you need to manage your time and resources carefully. Hiding in someone else's shadow—shadow hiding—was very popular during this time.

During this time of innovation for ninjas, a newly developed technique known as Hiya! made its first recorded appearance. Hiya! basically consists of choosing your striking point or general angle of death and then shouting "Hiya!" as you arrive for the blow. The simple brilliance of Hiya! is that it causes your enemy to actually assist you in killing them. The word *Hiya* is designed to unnerve and confuse its shoutee. It would take most creatures years to be able to counteract the Hiya! effect, and, quite honestly, most creatures are just too lazy to do so.

Before the Hiya! was introduced, ninjas would just shout anything or nothing at all as they landed a punch or a kick.

Banana!

Retroactive!

Shelving!

None of it made any sense, and very little of it was effective in causing an enemy to do anything but furrow his brow in confusion. On the other hand, Hiya! could cause an empusa† to turn her head into a triple temple kick or

---

* Large evil shadows that have the ability to physically interact with the physical world.

† Demonesses who bore people to death and then eat them (e.g., Renée Zellweger).

make a hippopotamuskrat* involuntarily bite down on a sword, driving its through its own head. The modern Hiya! used by ninjas today has changed very little from its original form. It is estimated that Hiya! has been the last thing heard by over 45 million creatures.

The Big Bam was in full swing and getting worse every day when, suddenly, *it happened.* A little girl started singing. No one can really explain why, but the fact is well documented and recounted by dozens of tribes of Killersapiens. It was a simple song and the girl was no older than six, but for some reason it made people, beasts, plants, and everything else pause. It is said that upon hearing the tiny girl's song, a giant killer whale spit back up an entire town perfectly intact. There are reports of lindworms becoming vegetarians, doppelgängers who stopped strangling each other, and yetis bathing . . . all due to the catchy tune of Meddy Simpson.

These are the lyrics to the unifying anthem that little Meddy wrote all by herself.

Why can't we all just get along
Why can't we all just sing this song
Today I saw a butterfly kiss a baby
It made me giggle, skip around and think that maybe
We could stop killin' each other in throngs

(CHORUS) You may say that I'm an unbelievably cute dreamer
And I might be the only one
I hope someday you will buy my album
And the world will be more fun

Now I believe in candy and pouting
Not eviscerating and shouting
Put down your swords, truncheons, and knives
Give back your torn-off limbs and gouged-out eyes
Hugs should be the only thing we're touting

CHORUS

I may only be adorable and six years old
But my blue eyes can still see

* The leading cause of death in urban Africa.

The intrinsic qualities of life in the known universe
Transcend why we disagree

CHORUS

The song, of course, ended the war and united the entire world. It became a time of unrivaled peace on Earth. Many called this time the Summer of Sex. It really seemed like everyone was doing it. Ninjas, although powerful and potent lovers, remained focused and continued to train and hone their skills and minds, knowing, of course, that no peace is an eternal one.

Meddy Simpson
are you looking at me?

Meddy's bestselling
debut album.

PROFILE: MEDDY SIMPSON

Meddy was born Medusa Rockstare Gorgon to Typhon and Echidna, the youngest of three girls who all showed artistic talents early on. Medusa and her sisters toured together as the Gorgonettes, but it was clear from the get-go that Medusa had star written all over her. Her very first solo single was the world-war ending "Cute Dreamer." After the song started catching on, her father/producer/creepy opportunist changed her name to something more catchy. However, without an immense bloody conflict as a backdrop, Meddy found it difficult to find a second hit. "Trouble with My S's" and "The Dimple Dance" barely made a blip on the ancient pop charts. One reviewer said of her Babylon concert, "A soon as young Miss Simpson took the stage, the audience froze and did not move for the rest of their lives." A few years later, her father dyed Meddy's snakes blond and tried to reinvent his little princess as an overtly sexual teen idol. Her back-to-back dance albums *Bone or Stone* and *Let's Bump Serpents* met with moderate success, but it was her tumultuous relationship with bad boy Poseidon that really kept her name in the papyrus. She retired at the age of 18, pregnant and strung out on crystal ambrosia. Sadly, a few months later she was beheaded in her sleep by an unknown assailant.

Great Conference of the Sentient

For the 70,004 years after the Summer of Sex, Earth lived under the philosophy of "Do whatever you want with whatever wants to do it with you."

At some point, this had to stop. Things were just getting too weird. Centaurs and griffins getting married were one thing, but the Homogriffosercentichtophibian Mountains (part eagle, part lion, part snake, part horse, part mackerel, part man, part mud puppy, part mountain things) were nearing metabiological insanity.

A poisonous flying multispecies mound of dirt was offensive and dangerous to everyone, even itself.

Because of this confusing combination and others, all of the life that existed gathered in what is modern-day Greenland and had it out. This meeting was called the Great Conference of the Sentient.

The meeting itself was surprisingly cordial and productive. The centaurs pledged to take it easy in the lust column, the really tweaked-out folks agreed to move to alternate planes of existence, and, at the request of the majority, the ninjas became the Universal Overseer of Respect and Honor, a calling that would unify the ninja community and heighten its commitment to awesomeness.

Hidden Millenniums

After the G.C.O.T.S., the ninjas were viewed as leaders and people that really had their shit together. Mostly, because they did. Many groups began to emulate the dark assassins as best as they could. This was the first time in history that black became cool . . . and it should be noted that the word *cool* didn't even exist yet. Everyone was wearing black. It was the new nothing. There had never been anything so widely accepted before. Black was the original black.

Although they will never admit this, before the Hidden Millenniums, pirates wore sea foam everything. That was their color. A sea foam flag with a coral-colored skull and crossbones.

No one took them seriously.

Then they switched to black. Whoa, Nelly. Suddenly, everyone is worried about the big bad pirates.

All in all, though, the Hidden Millenniums were a great time of peace and exploration among Killersapiens and Homo sapiens alike. When anyone would step out of line, the ninjas were there faster than you could say, "Hey, I need that organ."

Perhaps the greatest gift that the ninjas gave to the world during this period was a passion for sneakiness. It became almost a competition between the various tribes and species to see who could be most stealthy. The Amazons sunk their entire village of Atlantis into the ocean in an attempt to hide their training. Hobgoblins committed themselves to appearing only one day a year in the autumn to wreak their havoc, and even then they tried not to actually be seen by anyone.

There was one particular leviathan named Gevinerulshizgut that actually went quite mad with stealthiness. He bet a whale friend that he could hide undetected for a million years. A ninja, of course, found him in less than five minutes lying at the bottom of a lake in what is now Scotland, but he didn't have the heart to crush the aspirations of the crazed sea monster. The leviathan has yet to be "found" by anyone else.

The era was like a permission slip to be secretive. Nothing empowers a group like knowing that they know something that no other group knows. Just ask the Catholic Church or Colonel Sanders or a psychicat.*

This frenzy of hiding and sneaking did prove a great benefit to the Homo sapiens. They had, with no real effort on their part, a relatively safe and calm world in which to grow their civilizations. And grow they did. What they *did* with those civilizations is another story.

"Hey, let's capture a genie and put it in a bottle." A week after spending all its wishes on giant pyramids, the Egyptian empire was swallowed by sand.

"I think leprechauns will make great caged pets." Effect, the Irish Whiskey Famine.

Pompeii? "Why don't I build a town next to a volcano without asking the dragon that lives there."

The folks on Easter Island were wiped out by a poorly planed badminton tournament with quadruple elimination. It took so long to finish that everyone starved to death. Even today, Homo sapiens ignore the lessons of the past and continue to use oil for fuel, eat hot dogs, and live in California.

---

* Any of a number of felines with extrasensory perceptions whose knowledge can usually only be interpreted through careful analysis of their droppings.

Dark Ages

The Hidden Millenniums came to an end when the Killersapiens became so well hidden that existence itself couldn't find them. Everyone was still around, but no one was being seen. Hiding from people and nature is one thing, but Killersapiens were actually being forgotten by the collective unconscious, their archetypes slowly drifting into obscurity and rumor.

Ninjas were fine with this. Big public displays have never really been their thing. They have long considered themselves the Chris Cooper of assassins. Always there and doing their job perfectly, but never making a big flashy display.

Many other Killersapiens embraced the freedom of the darkness. Some did not.

Clowns, for example, could not bear it. The painted warriors could not stand being silent and secretive. The very core of their philosophy was the obnoxious embracing of color, sound, and movement. So in the early part of the Dark Ages, the clowns staged what became known as Wacko's Rebellion.

Twenty thousand clowns scattered across Earth embedded themselves as the premium jesters in 20,000 separate kingdoms, tribes, and children's hospitals. At 10:33 a.m. on April 1, the 20,000 clowns simultaneously told the exact same joke. What followed was the laugh heard around the world.

It was their way of separating themselves from the way of the ninja that had influenced Killersapiens for centuries. They were loud, they were proud, and everyone was going to have to get used to it.

From that point forward in history, clowns have stayed close to Homo sapiens, feeding off of their joy and laughter. Their manipulation and influence over regular people is incredible. That being said, they are still quite deadly. There are tales that Wacko the Whacker (for whom the rebellion is named) actually removed the internal organs of a Zhou dynasty emperor and juggled them in front of his face while the dying emperor laughed hysterically and cheered him on.

The Dark Ages are the time when most of the folklore and legends that now surround Killersapiens arose. Homo sapiens told stories of the bad old days, but each new generation had less and less actual interaction with Killersapiens, and those stories were gradually turned into myth.

Real events like the circumstances surrounding a creature named Grendel, his mother, his pet dragon, and some Scandinavian folks became stories. Stories that were rewritten to have people come out on top. The true story ended quite joyously with Grendel playing fetch with his dragon using the body of Beowulf while his mother prepared a horse-and-man casserole.

As the truth of history got distorted, some killer groups got upset. Several covens of witches and dens of wizards tried to "pull a clown" and integrate themselves into Homo sapien society. It would work for a generation or two, but then somebody would turn the wrong person into a newt or enchant the wrong sword and then WHOOSH . . . burned at the stake.

Even Darker Ages

It would seem that there can be nothing darker than being forgotten by existence, but there is. It is being eaten by the inverse totality of darkness. The inverse totality of darkness lies within the indefinable parameters of nothingness, far beyond the concept of existence. There it feeds off of nonexistence and the idea of absence. Every now and again, something that exists will fall so far off the radar of existence that it ends up on the dinner plate of the indefinable parameters of nothingness. That's what happened to several groups of Killersapiens, including ninjas.

At this point, the ninjas and fellow Killersapiens—including vikings, fairies, scorpion men, and vampires, to name a few—had to fight for the right to be. Since the battleground for nothingness is the abundant nonappearance of zero, it was tough to find good footing. All things that existed were quite useless. A sword is something, and somethings are quite irrelevant when you are trying to fight nothing.

The key in winning the battle was not to get that which existed to recognize your existence but rather to gain recognition from that which did not. By that, it should be understood that there was no simple solution. A ninja could not simply stand on top of a kitchen table banging on a pot with a soup ladle shouting, "I think, therefore I am." Ladles, pots, tables, and shouting exist. It was slightly much more complicated.

The final fix was developed by a very old ninja by the name of Red Death (yes, he was a descendent of the original Deaths). Old Red was thought by many to be quite off his katana. His first attempts at proposing his idea were met with great skepticism and kicking. Eventually, by persistence and pie baking, he was allowed to present his game plan to the Council of Shadows. The bid was simple but risky, just the way ninjas like it. It was also quite crazy. So crazy, they thought, that it just might work.

First, the ninjas picked a very obscure and relatively unknown weapon: the ashiko (spiked foot claws). The trick was to make the weapon not not not exist. Making something not not not exist is *not* the same as making something not exist or become extinct or destroyed. To not not not exist means that even the memory of existence doesn't remember that this thing existed. Since the ninjas were the only ones who knew about the ashiko, they started by physically, mentally, and spiritually removing all ashiko from existence. Then, much like in *Mission: Impossible II,* Old Red snuck into the Void of Reality and switched the connection feed that tells the indefinable parameters of nothingness that ashiko ever existed. Old Red, of course, died while doing this, because even if you sneak into the Void of Reality you are still in it. That means that you are no longer part of any reality. Including life.

After that, 1,066 ninjas meditated into a metaphysical chain that stretched from consciousness all the way to the indefinable parameters of nothingness. The last ninja in the line had no idea what to do once he was in the nothingness because, as was previously mentioned, all thoughts of ashiko had been eliminated. That ninja spent 200 years hanging there in that human chain. He actually had no idea why he was even doing it.

His life was in constant peril, for the indefinable parameters of nothingness contain everything that doesn't exist. That's a lot. We can't give you any examples because then they would exist, but believe me, they're double nasty. Thankfully, he was a ninja. He was able to fight, dodge, and slay all of the unknowable impediments he encountered. When he finally happened upon the "nonexistent" ashiko, he immediately recognized them as a weapon and mastered it. He attached them to his feet and ran with lightning speed across the fabric of antitime, punching tiny holes in it. Once enough time had seeped in, the indefinable parameters of nothingness realized it had a leak. It stopped up the holes and began drying out all of its nonexistent things. Not wanting to keep any of the warped, time-stained stuff for the fear that its place would start to smell like something, it packed up all the "damaged" items in a black hole and threw them into the known universe. One guess as to who was sitting on top of that black hole as it soared through the space-time continuum . . . a ninja.

Now, ninjas getting back into existence was a great thing, but we would be remiss if we didn't mention the slight new wrinkle that arose from the situation. Most of the other stuff that the indefinable parameters of nothingness threw out in the black hole had not previously existed, nor did they have any reason to. Some good things like cheese and a curveball entered reality. Some bad things like the U.S. Customary System of Measurement and mermecolions* were thrown in as well. And some just plain odd things like platypuses and suspense. The ninjas have done their best to rid the universe of these bad things. Mermecolions were pretty easy. The lion head would keep eating meat that the ant body couldn't digest. The U.S. Customary System of measurement is still one of our greatest foes.

Golden Age of Death

Many philosophinjas have attempted to comprehend the circumstances giving rise to the time known as the Golden Age of Death. So far, all have failed. But more important than its causes and reasons is the simple fact that it happened. The Golden Age of Death was an unrivaled period of honor, justice, advancement, and super kills. Living in this time was like having one of those days when everything you swing your sword at falls in one stroke, except that day lasted 400 years. It was during this time that the ninja excelled faster and more precisely than ever before. It really seemed as if everyone was foot, fist, and fancy free. It was a real good time. Ninja art, science, and culture reached new levels of astonishingness.

It is a time proudly reflected upon by ninjas. A bold statement to the ages that ninjas do not just hide, sneak, and kill, although we are extremely good at those things, but we also create, think, and kill. Here are just a scant few examples to illustrate the magnitude and diversity of ninja activity during the Golden Age of Death.

- **Painting.** The Moaning Lisa, Dirises, Femme avec les divises et le coeur enleve, A Sunday on La Grande (a.k.a. Where's Ninja?), Midsummer's Cleave, Starless Night, The Decapolade, Evisceration of Man, Madonna and Nunchucks.

- **Sculpture.** The Invisible David, The Thinking About Deather, Buddha, The Shuriken Thrower, The Kill. (After his masterful and perfectly accurate statue representing how he personally killed the goddess Venus was misinterpreted, the rather temperamental sculptor Stranglangelo made it his mission to chop off all of the heads, arms, and other pieces of non-ninja statues that weren't "good enough.")

* Half lion/half ants.

- **Plays.** McDeath, The Importance of Being Quiet, All's Well That Ends Horrifically, The Demiser, Who's Afraid of Virginja Woolf, The Stabday Party, The School for Knives.

- **Literature.** Bloody Expectations, To Kill an Anything, Paradise Gutted, The Sun Also Sets, On the Roadkill, No Sound All Fury, Extremely Dangerous Liaisons, The Brother's Killemalloff.

- **Music.** Beatallovem, Punchinni, Choppin', Johead Soonbashedin Back, Modart.

- **Science.** Transtemporal Physioflection provided a safe way to heal yourself quickly by connecting your mind with your future physical form after any would-be operations, recovery, and rehabilitation, and reflecting that state on your now current being. It was a simple idea, but one that had not been considered until this time. Sciencinjas also began to make detailed charts and lists of the attributes of each realm, dimension, and plane. The result was the Perniciodic Table, which is still required memorizing for all ninjas.

- **Techninlogy.** The Blacker Than Black Light revolutionized the way that ninjas lived. It gave them the ability to see more without being seen more. Digital Meditation allowed ninjas to violate core rules of string theory and move nonlinearly through planes of consciousness. The Wheel of Death, originally designed as a children's game, soon became a valuable tool for the hardworking ninja who didn't always have time to decide how to kill something. With a flick of the finger, the Wheel of Death would decide for you.

The Golden Age of Death is also sometimes referred to as the Rebirth of Pain. Many of the ripples from stones dropped during this period still spread through the modern ninja world. While the Homo sapien world was perfecting sexism, racism, and impractical clothing, ninjas were truly seeking the faceless face of an ultimate ninja. The true spirit of the times is very well exemplified in the following excerpt from the Killiam Bolding novel *Sword of the Flies*.

The boy with fair hair lowered himself down the last few feet of rock and began to pick his way toward the lagoon. He knew that was where the only sword to survive the crash was lying coldly in the sand, awaiting the hands of a righteous master. The young ninja could sense that whoever held the sword would not only be able to speak his mind freely but also cut out the tongues of those who acted like savage, insane idiots. By nightfall the heads of all of the bigguns were neatly placed on pikes facing into the forest. It was a clear message to anyone or anything on the island that might think about messing with the boy and his crew. The next order of business was building a fire.

Rise of the Machines

There is a tremendous battle raging. It has grown since the late 1400s, when the first artificial human-made intelligent beings were created. First was the Electrobrainwonderloom, invented by a madder than usual clown named Dr. Wobblepop. It was a walking, talking, and thinking weaving machine. It was foolish of clowns to think they would be able to control the thoughts of these creatures, and it wasn't long before these new life-forms turned on their "masters" and began weaving death.* Now, clowns, as you may recall, are very proud painted warriors who believe in hiding nothing. They admit to creating and losing control of the machines, but they are also quite convinced they can handle the situation.

Ninjas are not as confident, especially since the clowns have been quite unable to control the machines for over 600 years. In that time, machines, or robots, as they prefer to be called, have advanced at an alarming rate. They have developed the means for traveling through dimensions and planes of existence. You can only imagine how surprised the first ninja to come across a meditating robot in the Shadow Spirit Realm must have been. They have written elaborate programs that allow them to process thousands of senses and feelings. They know why you cry. They have amazing and clear definitions for love and hate. Born from reason rather than instinct, they have survived and progressed with logic rather than will. They are absolute in their dedication and open to all possibilities except doubt . . . and they are driven by a hatred for the living. Ninjas and other Killersapiens have repeatedly asked the robots why they hate organic life so much. We have only been

* Read *The Giant Electronic Shoes,* by Isbot Assibot.

informed that our minds are too illogical to comprehend their reason, but that it has something to do with cheese or chess.

Most Killersapiens have accepted that the robots are now much more powerful than the clowns. Both groups, however, have chosen to "ally" themselves with Homo sapiens in the hopes of dominating all of humanity. Ninjas regularly battled with clowns over this issue before there were robots and now must often battle both groups, sometimes at the same time. Robots are a key reason why ninjas are stealthy and prudent with their use of techninlogy. Ninjas rarely use electronics in their weaponry and invented a (so far) unhackable Ninternet, a worldswide ninja computer network that has access to every non-ninja computer, but is completely undetectable and impenetrable to outside electronics. Of course, the robots have their own separate secure network called S.A.L.L.Y.F.O.R.T.H., an acronym that has yet to be cracked.

Ninjas do not wish the eradication of any species real or artificial, but strive for balance, respect, and honor between all forces. Robots, however, have extincted several species and are consistently encouraging others to do the same. Have you ever heard a robot speak out against global warming? And you never will.

Currently, there are 4,272 machines for every sentient nonmachine lifeform on Earth (including skin mites).* They are truly humanity's greatest foe and are slowly trying to make Earth uninhabitable, choking off the resources for human sustenance and making it only sustainable for them . . . just like in the movies.

---

* Admittedly, mites' thoughts are small, like "Mmmm" and "Uhhhhh," but they're thoughts.

Thoughts of Finality from the Ask A Ninja Ninja

There is an old joke that goes "What is the last thing to go through a ninja's mind as he finishes writing a book for non-ninjas about ninjas?" The answer: "A flaming spear with a spiked ball attached to the tip." Get it? That joke, like most, was born from a series of very real events. But times change and species evolve. Is the non-ninja world ready for this book? I don't know, but I probably should have considered that at the beginning rather than now. If not, it will at least be a great push forward. I'm quite confident that the first generation to truly understand this manuscript will hail it as the best piece of literature ever to have been penned. The fact that I am largely responsible for its brilliant existence is just a cool bonus.

Here are a couple of leftover thoughts and ponderings to consider while I silently sneak up behind you.

Ninja is a way of doing anything while appearing to do nothing, of being all that you're not, but that you really are.

You cannot buy tickets to a ninja's show of force. His audience is his enemy. He walks with no swagger and to the beat of a silent drum.

Don't be stupid.

A ninja is not swayed by emotion or uncertainty and never questions the motives of his master.*

You can't trust a big butt and a smile.

If you're not already dead, I look forward to killing you soon.

---

* Unless it's something just crazy town like using a series of strongly worded letters to kill a boldfish (a very bold goldfish). Any intimidation that takes more than 11 seconds is useless on them.

GLOSSARY

GLOSSARY: A worthless inadequate tool for the weak. If you need something explained to you or defined for you, you do not have the ninja spirit. Life is meant to be lived. Go out and experience the things you need to know. Your answers lie in the actions you take. Hopefully, you will learn that even those definitions gained through experience are feeble. The whole of existence is in constant motion. Respect that even for something to stay the same is a form of change, for did not many other things change while that one thing stayed the same? Everything is always in flux. Lines and boxes are the leg braces of adventure. Once you break free from them, the true enterprise begins.

I AM NINJA!

ACKNOWLEDGMENTS

Douglas and Kent would like to acknowledge and thank the following:

The International Order of Ninjas for allowing us the honor of transcribing your magnificent and deadly wisdom

The Ask A Ninja ninja for not killing us

Mike "Hand of Death" Lea for his wonderfully twisted illustrations

Lan "Fire Eye" Bui and Vu "Blood Stare" Bui for their fliptastic photography

Barbara (a.k.a. Flying Pain), the Ninja's stealthy apprentice

Julian "Mighty Pen" Pavia and Three Rivers Press

Joe "Viper Fist" Veltre and Artists Literary Group

The Friends and Fans of www.askaninja.com

Pete Alcorn, Sarah Atwood, Bernie Burns, Chili, Del Close, Evolutionary Media Group PR, MaryPat Farrell, Freaks, G33ks, Andy Greenfield, Matt Hullum, Steve Joe, Lake Arrowhead, Gary Larson, Matt Lichtenberg and Level Four Business Management, Jack London, Steve Martin, Meat, Mitchell, Mom, Mosaic Media Group (John Elliott, Shasta Cross), Nerds, Barb and Alan Nichols, NINJAS, Mike O'Hara, Robert Palm, Brett Pearsons, Public Libraries, Red Bull (Thomas and Ellie), Bill Sarine, William and Karen Sarine, Shadows, Silverberg & Knupp LLP (Rob Rader, Marc Mayer), Scott Simpson, Robert and Sandy Snively, United Talent Agency (Jay Gassner, Larry Salz, Barrett Garese), the Webers, and the Webernet.

The Ask A Ninja ninja would like to thank you for reading this book and acknowledge that he looks forward to killing you soon. ☺